ST PAUL
PRAYER BOOK

ST PAUL PRAYER BOOK

St Pauls
Middlegreen, Slough SL3 6BT, United Kingdom
Moyglare Road, Maynooth, Co. Kildare, Ireland

© St Pauls 1993
ISBN 085439 420 6
Printed in the EEC by Society of St Paul, Athlone, Ireland

St Pauls is an activity of the priests and brothers of the Society of St Paul who proclaim the Gospel through the media of social communication

CONTENTS

Daily Prayers	7
General Prayers	19
Prayers to Jesus	29
Prayers to the Blessed Virgin Mary	43
Prayers to the Saints	49
Litanies	55
Rosary	67
Benediction	77
Stations of the Cross	81
Prayers from the Bible	97
Hymns	107
Latin Hymns	151
Index	171
Hymns (title of first line)	179

Acknowledgements

The Publishers wish to express their gratitude for permission to include copyright material in this book. Every effort has been made to trace owners of copyright material, and we hope that no copyright has been infringed. Pardon is sought and apology made if the contrary be the case, and a correction will be made in any reprint of this book.

The texts in the Bible Prayers and in the Rosary sections are from the New Revised Standard Version Bible, copyright © 1989, Division of Christian Education of the National Council of the Churches of Christ in the United States of America; and are used by kind permission.

Excerpts from the English translation of the Roman Missal, copyright © 1973, International Committee on English in the Liturgy, Inc. All right reserved.

The Apostles Creed, the Nicene Creed, and the English translation of the Gloria in excelsis, copyright © International Consultation on English Texts.

DAILY PRAYERS

The Sign of the Cross

In the name of the Father,
and of the Son,
and of the Holy Spirit. Amen.

The Lord's Prayer

Our Father,
who art in heaven,
hallowed be thy name;
thy kingdom come,
thy will be done on earth as it is in heaven.
Give us this day our daily bread;
and forgive us our trespasses
as we forgive those who trespass against us;
and lead us not into temptation,
but deliver us from evil. Amen.

The Hail Mary

Hail Mary, full of grace,
the Lord is with thee.
Blessed art thou among women,
and blessed is the fruit of thy womb, Jesus.
Holy Mary, Mother of God,
pray for us sinners,
now and at the hour of our death. Amen.

The Glory Be

Glory be to the Father,
  and to the Son,
  and to the Holy Spirit.
As it was in the beginning,
  is now, and ever shall be,
  world without end. Amen.

The Angelus

The angel of the Lord declared unto Mary,
and she conceived by the Holy Spirit.
Hail Mary.

Behold the handmaid of the Lord,
be it done unto me according to your word.
Hail Mary.

And the Word was made flesh,
and dwelt among us.
Hail Mary.

Pray for us, O Holy Mother of God,
that we may be made worthy of the promises of Christ.

Let us pray. Pour forth, we beseech you, O Lord, your grace into our hearts, that we to whom the incarnation of Christ, your Son, was made known by the message of an angel, may, by his passion and cross, be brought to the glory of his resurrection. Through the same Christ our Lord. Amen.

The Regina Coeli

This prayer replaces the *Angelus* from the Easter Vigil until the evening of Pentecost Sunday.

Queen of heaven, rejoice, alleluia!
For he whom you did merit to bear, alleluia!
Has risen, as he said, alleluia!
Pray for us to God, alleluia!
Rejoice and be glad, O Virgin Mary, alleluia!
For the Lord has truly risen, alleluia!

Let us pray. O God, who has given joy to the world through the resurrection of your Son, our Lord Jesus Christ, grant that we may obtain, through his Virgin Mother, Mary, the joys of everlasting life. Through the same Christ our Lord. Amen.

Prayer of Adoration

I believe, my God,
    that I am in your presence,
    that you are looking at me
    and listening to my prayers.
You are so great and so holy:
    I adore you.
You have given me all:
    I thank you.
You have been so offended by me:
    I ask your pardon with all my heart.
You are so merciful:
    I ask of you all the graces which you
        know are beneficial to me.

To the Guardian Angel

O angel of God, appointed by divine mercy to be my guardian, enlighten and protect, direct and govern me this day. Amen.

Morning Prayer

O my God, I adore you,
   and I love you with all my heart.
I thank you for having created me
   and saved me by your grace,
     and for having preserved me during the night.
I offer you all my prayers,
   works, joys and sufferings of this day.
Grant that they may be all according to
   your will
   and for your great glory.
Keep me from all sin and evil,
   and may your grace be always with me
   and with those I love. Amen.

The Apostles' Creed

I believe in God, the Father almighty,
   creator of heaven and earth.

I believe in Jesus Christ, his only Son, our Lord.
   He was conceived by the power of the
     Holy Spirit
   and born of the Virgin Mary.

He suffered under Pontius Pilate,
   was crucified, died, and was buried.
He descended to the dead.
On the third day he rose again.
He ascended into heaven,
   and is seated at the right hand of the
      Father.
He will come again to judge the living and
   the dead.

I believe in the Holy Spirit,
   the holy catholic Church,
   the communion of saints,
   the forgiveness of sins,
   the resurrection of the body,
   and the life everlasting. Amen.

The Nicene Creed

We believe in one God,
   the Father, the Almighty,
   maker of heaven and earth,
   of all that is, seen and unseen.

We believe in one Lord, Jesus Christ,
   the only Son of God,
   eternally begotten of the Father,
   God from God, Light from Light,
   true God from true God,
   begotten, not made,
   of one Being with the Father.
   Through him all things were made.

For us men and for our salvation
> he came down from heaven:
by the power of the Holy Spirit
> he became incarnate from the
> Virgin Mary, and was made man.
For our sake he was crucified under
> Pontius Pilate;
>> he suffered death and was buried.
On the third day he rose again
> in accordance with the Scriptures;
he ascended into heaven
> and is seated at the right hand of the
> Father.
He will come again in glory to judge the
> living and the dead,
> and his kingdom will have no end.

We believe in the Holy Spirit, the Lord,
> the giver of life,
> who proceeds from the Father and the Son.
With the Father and the Son he is
> worshipped and glorified.
He has spoken through the Prophets.
We believe in only holy catholic and
> apostolic Church.
We acknowledge one baptism for the
> forgiveness of sins.
We look for the resurrection of the dead,
> and the life of the world to come. Amen.

An Act of Faith

O my God, I firmly believe that you are one God in three divine persons: Father, Son, and Holy Spirit; I believe that your divine Son became man and died for our sins, and that he will come to judge the living and the dead. I believe these and all the truths which the holy catholic Church teaches, because you have revealed them who can neither deceive nor be deceived.

An Act of Hope

O my God, relying on your infinite goodness and promises I hope to obtain pardon of my sins, the help of your grace, and life everlasting, through the merits of Jesus Christ, my Lord and Redeemer.

An Act of Love

O my God, I love you above all things, with my whole heart and soul, because you are all good and worthy of all love. I love my neighbour as myself for the love of you. I forgive all who have injured me and I ask pardon of all whom I have injured.

An Act of Contrition

O my God, I am heartily sorry for having offended you, and I detest all my sins, because of your just punishment, but most of all because they offend you, my God, who are all good and deserving of all my love. I firmly resolve, with the help of your grace, to sin no more and to avoid the near occasions of sin.

The Gloria

Glory to God in the highest
   and peace to his people on earth.

Lord God, heavenly King,
almighty God and Father,
   we worship you, we give you thanks,
   we praise you for your glory.

Lord Jesus Christ, only Son of the Father,
Lord God, Lamb of God,
you take away the sin of the world:
   have mercy on us;
you are seated at the right hand of the Father:
   receive our prayer.

For you alone are the Holy One,
you alone are the Lord,
you alone are the Most High,
   Jesus Christ,
   with the Holy Spirit,
   in the glory of God the Father. Amen.

Grace before Meals

Bless us, O Lord,
and these your gifts
which we are about to receive from your
   bounty.
Through Christ our Lord. Amen.

Grace after Meals

We give you thanks, almighty God,
for all your benefits,
who live and reign
for ever and ever. Amen.

Before Work

Lord God, King of heaven and earth,
guide, direct and sanctify our hearts,
our bodies, our senses,
all our words and work today. Amen.

Before Study

Father, let your Holy Spirit come upon me and fill me with wisdom and understanding so that I may know and do your will. I ask you this through Christ our Lord. Amen.

Before Reading the Bible

Lord, may your Sacred Scripture be my delight.
Let me praise you for all the truths I discover
   in these sacred books.
Help me to listen to the voice of the Spirit:
   refresh me as I meditate on the wonders
      of your law.

After Reading the Bible

Lord, you have words of eternal life.
   I adore you, I praise you,
   I beseech you, and I thank you
      for the gift of Sacred Scripture.

Prayer to Jesus Christ

Lord Jesus Christ,
   take all my freedom,
   my memory, my understanding, my will.
All that I have and cherish you have given me.
   I surrender it all to be guided by your will.
Your grace and your love are wealth enough
   for me.
Give me these, Lord Jesus, and I ask for
   nothing more.

St Ignatius Loyola

Prayer to the Holy Spirit

Come, O Holy Spirit, fill the hearts of your
  faithful, and kindle in them the fire of
    your love.
  Send forth your Spirit and they shall be
    created.
  And you shall renew the face of the earth.

O God, who has taught the hearts of the faithful by the light of the Holy Spirit, grant that by the gifts of the same Spirit we may always be truly wise and ever rejoice in his consolation. Through Christ our Lord. Amen.

Prayer for Final Perseverance

Our dear Redeemer,
  relying on your promises,
  because you are faithful, all-powerful,
    and merciful,
  we hope,
  through the merits of your passion,
  for the forgiveness of our sins,
  perseverance until death in your grace;
  and at length we hope,
  by your mercy,
  to see and love you eternally in heaven.

St Alphonsus Liguori

Prayer for a Happy Death

Father, you made us in your own image, and your Son accepted death for our salvation. Help us to keep watch in prayer at all times. May we be free from sin when we leave this world and rejoice in peace with you for ever. Amen.

The Confiteor

I confess to almighty God,
and to you, my brothers and sisters,
that I have sinned through my own fault
in my thoughts and in my words,
in what I have done,
and in what I have failed to do;
and I ask blessed Mary, ever virgin,
all the angels and saints,
and you, my brothers and sisters,
to pray for me to the Lord our God.

Night Prayer

O my God, I adore you, and I love you with all my heart. I thank you for having created me and saved me by your grace, and for having preserved me during this day. I pray that you will take for yourself whatever good I might have done this day and that you will forgive me whatever evil I have done. Protect me this night, and may your grace be always with me and with those I love. Amen.

GENERAL PRAYERS

To God the Father

God be in my head
    and in my understanding.
God be in mine eyes
    and in my looking.
God be in my mouth
    and in my speaking.
God be in my heart
    and in my thinking.
God be at my end
    and at my departing.

Book of Hours (1514)

Deliver us, Lord, from every evil,
and grant us peace in our day.
in your mercy keep us free from sin
and protect us from all anxiety
as we wait in joyful hope
for the coming of our Saviour, Jesus Christ.

For love of neighbour

Loving Father, our Creator,
    teach us to love our brothers and sisters
    of every age, nation, race and colour.

Give us the grace
    to obey the words of Jesus, who said,
    'Love one another as I have loved you.'
Give us, Father, the grace
    to understand the sufferings of others
    as we understand our own.
Bestow on us
    the gift of true brotherhood.
Help us, Father, to work together
    to make the world a place where you will be
    adored by all your people in peace and joy.

Prayer for sharing

Almighty and eternal God,
    may your grace enkindle in all of us
    a love for the many unfortunate people
    whom poverty and misery reduce
    to a condition of life unworthy of human
        beings.

For peace and justice

Make us worthy, Lord,
to serve others throughout the world
who live and die in poverty and hunger.
Give them through our hands
this day
their daily bread,
and by our understanding love,
give peace and joy.

Mother Teresa of Calcutta

For community spirit

O God,
teach us to live together
in love and joy and peace,
to check all bitterness,
to disown discouragement,
to practise thanksgiving,
and to leap with joy to any task for others.
Strengthen the good thing thus begun,
that with gallant and high-hearted happiness
we may look for your kingdom.
Through Jesus Christ.

The Prayer of Toc H

For work

Father,
you have called men and women,
through their daily work,
to share in your work of creation.
May we recognize others as our brothers
    and sisters
and, by the power of your Spirit,
strive with them for a more just world
where men and women will find work
in accordance with the dignity of their
    vocation,
and will contribute
to the progress of all nations.

For prisoners

God of mercy,
the secrets of all hearts
are known to you alone.
You know who is just,
and you forgive the unjust.
Hear our prayers for those in prison.
Give them patience and hope
in their sufferings,
and bring them home again soon.

For refugees

Lord,
no one is a stranger to you
and no one is ever far
from your loving care.
In your kindness
watch over the refugees and exiles,
those separated from their loved ones,
young people who are lost,
and those who have left
or run away from home.
Bring them back safely
to the place where they long to be,
and help us always to show your kindness
to strangers and those in need.

For the homeless

Have mercy, O Lord our God,
on those whom
>war or oppression or famine
>robbed of homes and friends,
>and sustain all those who try to help them.

We commend also into your care
>those whose homes are broken
>by conflict and lack of love;

grant that where human love has failed,
>your compassion may heal.

For the handicapped

O loving Father,
we pray for all who are handicapped in life:
>the blind, the defective and the delicate,
>and all who are permanently injured.

We pray for those worn out with sickness
>and those who are wasted with misery,
>for the dying,
>and all unhappy children.

May they learn the mystery of the road of suffering
>which Christ has trodden
>and the saints have followed,

and bring you this gift that angels cannot bring,
>a heart that trusts you even in the dark;

and this we ask
> in the name of him who himself
> took our infirmities upon him,
> the same Jesus Christ, our Saviour.

A.S.T. Fisher

For the Church

Father,
in the new covenant instituted by Christ,
> your Son,
you gather your people
in the unity of the Spirit
from all the nations of the earth.
Keep your Church faithful to her mission
as a leaven in the world,
renewing all peoples in Christ
and transforming them into your own family.

For the local Church

Father,
in every local Church you show forth
your one holy catholic and apostolic Church.
Gathered around its shepherd
may this family grow
in love and unity of the Holy Spirit
through the Gospel and the Eucharist.
Make us become true witnesses
to the presence of Christ in the world.

For the Pope

Lord, source of eternal life and truth,
give our Holy Father the Pope
a spirit of courage and right judgement,
a spirit of knowledge and love.
By governing with fidelity those entrusted to his care may he,
as successor to the apostle Peter and vicar of Christ,
build your Church into a sacrament of unity,
love and peace for all the world.

For persecuted Christians

Father,
in your mysterious providence,
your Church is called to share
in the sufferings of Christ, your Son.
Give the spirit of endurance and love
to those who are persecuted for their faith
in you.
May they always be true and faithful witnesses
to your promise of eternal life.

For Christian unity

Lord,
pour out upon us the fullness of your mercy,
and by the power of your Spirit
remove divisions among Christians.

Let your Church rise more clearly
as a sign for all the nations,
that the world may be filled
with the light of your Spirit
and believe in Jesus Christ
whom you have sent.

For the missions

God of truth,
Father, Son, and Holy Spirit,
    hear our prayer for those who do not
        know you,
    that your name may be praised
    among all peoples of the world.
Sustain and inspire your servants
    who bring them the Gospel.
Bring fresh vigour to wavering faith;
    sustain our faith when it is fragile.
Renew our missionary zeal.
Make us witnesses to your goodness,
    full of love, strength and faith,
    for your glory,
    and for the salvation of the world.

For vocations

Jesus, eternal Shepherd of our souls,
    send good labourers into your harvest.

For our country

Lord God,
you guide the universe with wisdom and love.
Hear the prayer we make to you for our country:
    Through the honesty of our citizens
    and the wisdom of those who govern
    may concord and justice flourish
    and lasting peace be achieved.

For civil authorities

Almighty and ever living God,
in whose hands are the rights and hopes of everyone,
look graciously on those who govern,
that in lasting peace
they may promote social progress and religious freedom
for all the nations of the earth.

Prayer for the media apostolate

God, to communicate your love to all
    you sent your only Son, Jesus Christ,
        into the world
    and made him our Life.
Grant that the media of social communication
    may always be used for your glory
    and the good of all.

Raise up vocations for this apostolate,
    and inspire all people of goodwill
    to contribute with prayer and work,
so that through these means
    the Church may proclaim the Gospel
    to all peoples.

For the dead

Eternal rest give unto them, O Lord,
and let perpetual light shine upon them.
May they rest in peace. Amen.

The Master's way

Not ours to know the reason why,
Unanswered is our prayer,
But ours to wait for God's own time
To life the cross we bear;
Not ours to know the reason why
From loved ones we must part,
But ours to live in faith and hope,
Though bleeding to the heart;
Not ours to know the reason
Why this anguish, strife and pain,
But ours to know a crown of thorns
Sweet graces for us gain,
A cross, a bleeding heart and crown
What greater gifts are given?
Be still, my heart, and murmur not;
These are the Keys of Heaven.

PRAYERS TO JESUS

Come, my Way, my Truth, my Life:
    Such a Way as gives us breath,
    Such a Truth as ends all strife,
    Such a Life as killeth death.

George Herbert

Lord Jesus Christ, Son of the living God,
teach us to walk in your Way more trustfully,
to accept your Truth more faithfully,
and to share your Life more lovingly.

By the power of the Holy Spirit
help us in our works for the Church
so that we may come as one family
to the kingdom of the Father,
where you live for ever and ever.

Jesus, Divine Master,
we adore you as the Word Incarnate
sent by the Father
to instruct us in life-giving truth.
You are uncreated Truth, the only Master.
You alone have words of eternal life.
We thank you for having ignited in us
the light of reason and the light of faith,
and for having called us to the light of glory.

Master,
show us the treasures of your wisdom,
let us know the Father,
makes us your true disciples.
Increase our faith,
so that we may attain to the eternal vision
 in heaven.

Christ be near at either hand,
   Christ behind, before me stand,
Christ with me where e'er I go,
   Christ around, above, below.

Christ be in my heart and mind,
   Christ within my soul enshrined.
Christ control my wayward heart;
   Christ abide and ne'er depart.

Christ my life and only way,
   Christ my lantern night and day;
Christ be my unchanging friend,
   Guide and shepherd to the end.

Canon J. Fennelly

Lord Jesus,
I give you my hands to do your work.
I give you my feet to go your way.
I give you my eyes to see as you do.
I give you my tongue to speak your words.

I give you my mind that you may think in me.
I give you my spirit that you may pray in me.

Above all, I give you my heart
　that you may love in me
　your Father and all humankind.
I give you my whole self that you may grow
　　in me,
　so that it is you, Lord Jesus,
　who live and work and pray in me.

Grail Prayer

Teach us, good Lord,
to serve you as you deserve;
to give and not to count the cost,
to fight and not to heed the wounds,
to toil and not to seek for rest,
to labour and not ask for any reward,
　save that of knowing that we do your will.

St Ignatius

O blessed Jesus,
make me understand and remember
　that whatsoever we gain,
　　if we lose you, all is lost,
　and whatsoever we lose,
　　if we gain you, all is gained.

St Thomas Cottam

Lord, make me an instrument of your peace:
> where there is hatred, let me sow love;
> where there is injury, let me sow pardon;
> where there is doubt, let me sow faith;
> where there is despair, let me give hope;
> where there is darkness, let me give light;
> where there is sadness, let me give joy.

O Divine Master, grant that I may try
> not to be comforted, but to comfort;
> not to be understood, but to understand;
> not to be loved, but to love.

Because it is in giving that we receive,
it is in forgiving that we are forgiven,
and it is in dying that we are born to eternal life.

St Francis of Assisi

Give me, good Lord,
a full faith and a fervent charity,
a love of you, good Lord,
incomparable above the love of myself;
and that I love nothing to your displeasure
but everything in an order to you.

Take from me, good Lord,
this lukewarm fashion,
or rather key-cold manner of meditation

and this dullness in praying to you.
And give me warmth, delight and life
in thinking about you.
And give me your grace
to long for your holy sacraments
and specially to rejoice
in the presence of your blessed Body,
sweet Saviour Christ,
in the holy Sacrament of the altar,
and duly to thank you
for your gracious coming.

St Thomas More

Soul of Christ, sanctify me.
Body of Christ, save me.
Blood of Christ, inebriate me.
Water from the side of Christ, wash me.
Passion of Christ, strengthen me.
O good Jesus, hear me.
Within your wounds hide me.
Permit me not to be separated from you.
From the malignant enemy defend me.
In the hour of my death call me.
And bid me come to you,
That with your saints I may praise you
for ever and ever.

Lord, give me patience in tribulation.
Let the memory of your Passion,
and of those bitter pains you suffered for me,
strengthen my patience
and support me
in this tribulation and adversity.

St John Forrest

Thanks be to you, my Lord Jesus Christ,
> for all the benefits which you have given me,
> for all the pains and insults
> which you have borne for me.

O most merciful Redeemer, Friend and Brother,
> may I know you more clearly,
> love you more dearly,
> follow you more nearly,
> day by day.

St Richard of Chichester

Prayer of self-dedication to Jesus Christ

Lord Jesus Christ,
> take all my freedom,
> my memory, my understanding, and my will.

All that I have and cherish you have given me.
> I surrender it all to be guided by your will.
> Your grace and your love are wealth enough
>   for me.

Give me these, Lord Jesus, and I ask for
nothing more.

Prayer before the Blessed Sacrament

You know better than I
   how much I love you, Lord.
You know it and I know it not,
   for nothing is more hidden from me
   than the depths of my own heart.
I desire to love you;
I fear that I do not love you enough.
I beseech you to grant me the fullness of pure love.
Behold my desire;
   you have given it to me.
Behold in your creature
   what you have placed there.
O God, who love me enough
   to inspire me to love you for ever,
   behold not my sins.
Behold your mercy and my love.

François Fénelon

Set our hearts on fire with love to thee,
O Christ our God,
that in that flame
we may love thee with all our heart,
with all our mind,
with all our soul,
and with all our strength,
and our neighbour as ourselves;

so that, keeping thy commandments,
we may glorify thee,
the giver of all good gifts.

Eastern Orthodox Prayer

♦

Use me, my Saviour,
> for whatever purpose and in whatever way
> > thou mayest require.

Here is my poor heart, an empty vessel;
> fill it with thy grace.

Here is my sinful, troubled soul;
> quicken it and refresh it with thy love.

Take my heart for thine abode;
> my mouth to spread abroad the glory of
> > thy name;

my love and all my powers
> for the advancement of thy believing people,

and never suffer the steadfastness and
> confidence of my faith to abate.

Dwight Moody

♦

Be thou a light unto my eyes,
> music to mine ears,
> sweetness to my taste
> and full contentment to my heart.

Be thou my sunshine in the day,
> my food at table,

my repose in the night,
my clothing in nakedness,
and my succour in all necessities.
Lord Jesus,
I give thee my body, my soul,
my substance, my fame, my friends,
my liberty and my life.
Dispose of me and all that is mine
as it may seem best to thee
and to the glory of thy blessed name.

John Cosin

◆

O Lord and Master of my life,
banish from me
all idleness and discouragement,
and all thirst for power and glory.
Grant me instead, O Lord,
the spirit of chastity,
humility, patience and love.

Make me see,
I beseech you, O Lord,
my countless faults,
and teach me
not to judge my brothers and sisters,
for you alone are the Lord and Master
for ever and ever.

St Ephrem

Prayer before Mass

Lord Jesus Christ,
I approach your banquet table
in fear and trembling,
for I am a sinner and dare not rely on my worth
but only on your goodness and mercy.
I am defiled by my sins in body and soul
and by my unguarded thoughts and words.

Gracious God of majesty and awe,
I seek your protection,
I look for your healing.
Poor troubled sinner that I am,
I appeal to you, the fountain of all mercy.
I cannot bear your judgement,
but I trust in your salvation.
Lord, I show my wounds to you
and uncover my shame before you.
I know my sins are many and great,
and they fill me with fear,
but I hope in your mercies,
for they cannot be numbered.

Lord Jesus Christ, eternal king, God and man,
crucified for humankind,
look upon me with mercy and hear my prayer,
for I trust in you.
Have mercy on me,
full of sorrow and sin,
for the depth of your compassion never ends.

Praise to you, saving sacrifice,
offered on the wood of the cross for me
   and for all humankind.
Praise to the noble and precious blood,
flowing from the wounds of my crucified
   Lord Jesus Christ,
and washing away the sins of the whole world.

Remember, Lord, your creature,
whom you have redeemed with your blood.
I repent my sins,
and I long to put right what I have done.
Merciful Father, take away all my offences
   and sins;
purify me in body and soul,
and make me worthy to taste the holy of holies.
May your body and blood,
which I intend to receive, although I am
   unworthy,
be for me the remission of my sins,
the washing away of my guilt,
the end of my evil thoughts,
and the rebirth of my better instincts.
May it incite me to do the works pleasing to you
and profitable to my health in body and soul,
and be a firm defence
against the wiles of my enemies. Amen.

St Ambrose

Prayer before a Crucifix

Behold, my beloved and good Jesus,
I cast myself upon my knees in your sight,
and with the most fervent desire of my soul,
I pray and beseech you to impress upon
　my heart
lively sentiments of faith, hope and charity,
with a true repentance for my sins
and a firm desire of amendment,
while with deep affection and grief of soul
I ponder within myself and mentally
　contemplate
your five most precious wounds,
having before my eyes
that which David spoke in prophecy of you,
　O good Jesus:
'They have pierced my hands and my feet;
they have numbered all my bones.'

Eucharistic offering

Lord,
all that is in heaven and on earth is yours.
I wish to offer myself up to you
as a voluntary sacrifice
and to remain always yours.
Lord,
in the simplicity of my heart,
I offer myself to you today
as a perpetual servant,

for a homage and sacrifice of eternal praise
> to you.
Receive me
with this holy oblation of your precious body,
which I offer to you this day,
in the presence of your angels,
that it may be a salvation for me
and for all the people.

Imitation of Christ

Hymn to Christ

Christ, in thee I do believe,
> thou who all our pains relieve.
Come, protect and help me, Lord,
> while I labour for thy word.
Hasten to my help, I pray,
> bear my burden every day.
Thou the maker of mankind,
> place in heav'n for all men find.

Christ who loves the virgin choir,
> Christ, redeemer from hell-fire,
fount of wisdom, pure and clear,
> in whose word we hope and fear.

Christ, our guard at hour of fight,
> Christ, who made the world and light,
Christ, who crowns each conquering soul,
> count us in the heav'nly roll.

St Columba

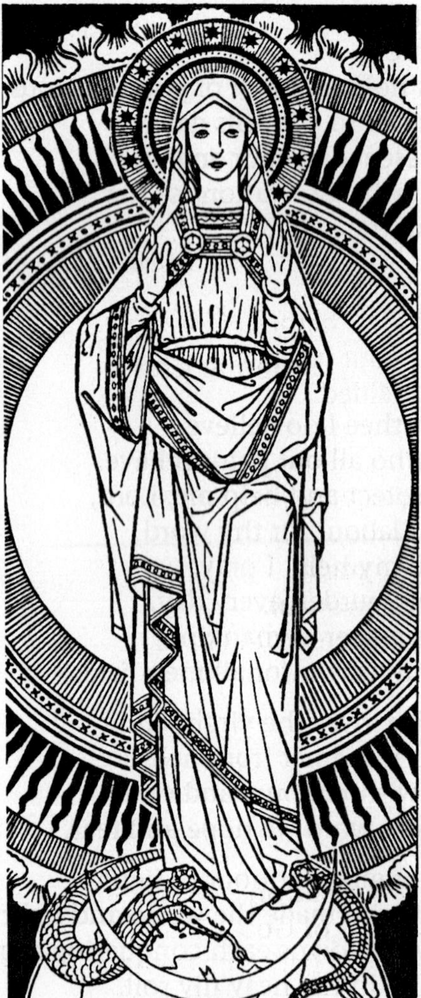

PRAYERS TO THE BLESSED VIRGIN MARY

The Memorare

Remember, O most gracious Virgin Mary,
that never was it known
that anyone who fled to your protection,
implored your help,
or sought your intercession
was left unaided.
Inspired with this confidence,
I fly to you,
O Virgin of virgins, my Mother.
To you I come,
before you I stand,
sinful and sorrowful.
O Mother of the Word Incarnate!
Despise not my petitions,
but in your mercy
hear and answer me. Amen.

We fly to your patronage

We fly to your patronage,
O holy Mother of God.
Despise not our petitions in our necessities,
but deliver us from all dangers,
O ever glorious and blessed Virgin.

Hail, Holy Queen

Hail, holy Queen, Mother of mercy.
Hail, our life, our sweetness, and our hope.
To you do we cry, poor banished children
 of Eve.
To you do we send up our sighs,
 mourning and weeping in this valley of tears.
Turn then, most gracious advocate,
 your eyes of mercy towards us,
 and after this our exile,
 show unto us the blessed fruit of your womb,
  Jesus.
O clement, O loving, O sweet Virgin Mary.

Prayer to Our Lady of Lourdes

O ever immaculate Virgin,
Mother of mercy, health of the sick,
refuge of sinners, comforter of the afflicted,
you know my needs, my troubles, my sufferings;
look with pity upon me.
By appearing in the Grotto of Lourdes,
you made it a privileged sanctuary.
With unbounded confidence
I implore your motherly intercession.
In gratitude for your favours,
I will endeavour to imitate your virtues
and I pray that one day I may see your glory.

Prayer to Our Lady of Perpetual Succour

O Mother of Perpetual Succour,
   behold me a miserable sinner at your feet.
I have recourse to you and put my trust in you.
O Mother of Mercy, have pity upon me.
Be my refuge and my hope.
Succour me for the love of Jesus.
Stretch forth your hand to me a poor sinner.
I bless and thank God
   for giving me confidence in you,
   the pledge of my eternal salvation.
Too often I have miserably fallen
   because I did not have recourse to you.
I know that with your help I shall conquer.
This then is the grace I seek from you:
   in times of temptation
   help me to have recourse to you.

Prayer to Mary, Queen of the Apostles

Immaculate Mary,
look upon the human race,
redeemed by the blood of your divine Son,
yet still immersed in the darkness of error
and the mire of vice.
Have pity upon your children
whom the dying Jesus entrusted
to you from the cross.
Sustain with your motherly care
all who consecrate their lives

to the good of their neighbour.
Renew again the divine Pentecost
upon all those called to the apostolate.
Guide us all in our efforts;
help us with your graces;
sustain us in moments of discouragement;
crown our zeal with success.
Queen of Apostles, pray for us.

To the Immaculate Heart of Mary

O Temple of light without shadow or stain,
intercede for us with your only-begotten Son,
the mediator of our reconciliation with
　　the Father.
May our weaknesses be forgiven,
discord be rooted out of our hearts,
and may we know the joy
of loving our brothers and sisters.
O Mary, we commend the whole human race
to your Immaculate Heart;
may all peoples know
the one true Saviour, Jesus Christ;
may the consequences of sin
be washed away by his precious blood,
and may the whole world find peace
in truth, justice, freedom and love.

O Virgin,
who, begetting Christ,
have redeemed the human race,

offer to the ear of God
the prayers of those who invoke you.
You, who without corruption
begot the Saviour of all,
intercede for us
and obtain from the Lord,
joy and pardon for our sins.

Visigothic Book of Prayer

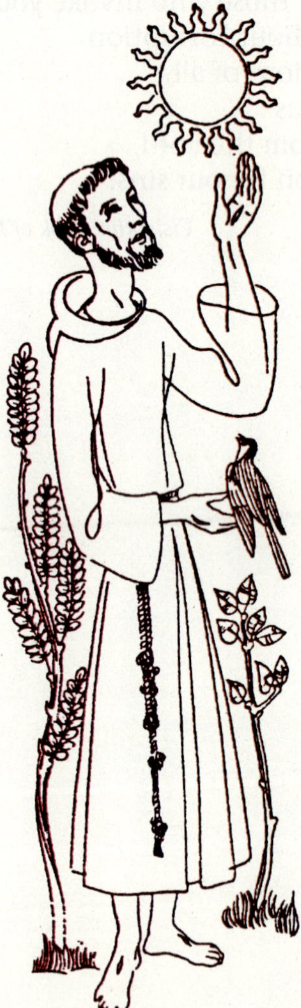

PRAYERS TO THE SAINTS

Prayer to St Joseph

To you, O blessed Joseph,
we fly in our tribulation
and, after imploring the help of your
    holy Spouse,
with confidence we also ask for your
    intercession.
By the affection
which united you to the Immaculate Virgin,
and by the fatherly love
with which you embraced the child Jesus,
we beseech you
to look kindly upon the inheritance
which Jesus Christ acquired
by his precious blood,
and with your powerful aid
to help us in our needs.
Protect,
most careful guardian of the Holy Family,
the chosen people of Jesus Christ.
Keep us, loving father,
from all pestilence of error and corruption.
From your place in heaven
be with us, most powerful protector,
in this warfare with the powers of darkness;
and as you once rescued the child Jesus
    from danger,

so now defend the holy Church of God
from the snares of the enemy and from
    all adversity.
Guard each of us by your constant patronage
so that, sustained by your example and help,
we may lead a holy life,
die a holy death,
and obtain the everlasting happiness
    of heaven.

Prayer to St Anthony

O wondrous Saint Anthony,
who had the happiness of receiving
within your arms Our Blessed Lord
under the guise of a little child,
obtain for me of his bounty
the favour I now ask of you…
You were always gracious to poor sinners;
do not look on my sinfulness,
but consider the glory of God
and my salvation.
As a pledge of my gratitude,
I resolve to be more faithful to God
every day of my life,
and to be devoted
to the service of the poor
whom you so greatly loved.
Bless this resolution,
and obtain for me the favour I so ardently
    desire.

Prayer to St Brigid

Dear Saint Brigid,
true witness to our faith
in its early days in Ireland,
we look up to you now in earnest prayer.
By your glorious sacrifice
of earthly riches, joys and affections,
obtain for us the grace
to seek first the kingdom of God
and his justice.
By your life of charity to the poor,
make us also true helpers of God.
By the peace of your death bed,
may we receive the fullness of pardon and peace
at the hour of our death.

Prayer to St Jude

O glorious Apostle Saint Jude,
  you were a close relative of Jesus and Mary.
I praise and thank God
  for all the grace he bestowed upon you.
I humbly implore you
  to look down upon me with compassion.
Despise not my poor prayer,
  let not my trust be confounded.
To you God has granted the privilege of aiding
  everyone in the most desperate cases.
Come to my aid,
  that I may praise the mercies of God.

Prayer to St Martin

Most humble Saint Martin,
whose burning charity embraces all,
but especially those who are
sick, afflicted, or in need.
We turn to you for help
in our present difficulties
and we implore you to obtain for us from God
health of soul and body,
and in particular the favour we now ask…
May we, by imitating your charity and
  humility,
find quiet and contentment all our days,
and cheerful submission to God's will
in all the trials and difficulties of life.

Prayer to St Oliver Plunkett

Glorious martyr, Saint Oliver Plunkett,
who willingly gave your life for the faith,
help us also to be strong in our faith.
By your intercession and example
may all hatred and bitterness be banished
from the hearts of men and women.
May the peace of Christ reign in our hearts
as it did in your heart
even at the moment of your death.

Prayer to St Patrick

O Saint Patrick, Apostle of Ireland,
submit to God our Father
our every temporal and spiritual need,
that through your intercession,
we may find help in all our necessities.
Obtain for us the grace that we may be found
worthy of our faith and of eternal salvation.

Prayer to St Paul the Apostle

O Holy Apostle,
who with your teaching and with your charity
taught the entire world,
look kindly upon us.
Pray for us that we may live by faith,
be saved by hope,
and that charity alone reign in us.
Obtain for us the grace
to correspond to the divine will
and that God's grace may not
remain unfruitful in us.
May we better know you and imitate you.
May the warm breath of true charity
permeate the entire world.
May all know and glorify God and Jesus,
the Divine Master, Way, Truth, and Life.

Prayer to St Rita

O glorious Saint Rita, you shared miraculously in the sorrowful passion of Our Lord Jesus Christ, obtain for me, that I may bear with resignation the sufferings of this life, and protect me in all my necessities.

O God, you bestowed on Saint Rita, the special grace to imitate you in love towards her enemies, bearing in her heart and on her face the marks of your love and passion, I beg of you to grant me through her intercession and merits to love my enemies and to keep the sufferings of your passion continually in my mind.

Prayer to St Teresa of the Child Jesus

O Saint Teresa of the Child Jesus, during your short life on earth you became a mirror of angelic purity, of love strong as death, and of wholehearted abandonment to God. Listen to my prayer. Speak a word for me to Our Lady Immaculate, the Queen of Heaven 'who smiled on you at dawn of life.' Beg her to obtain for me, by her powerful intercession, the grace I yearn for so ardently at this moment. And beg her to join with it a blessing that may strengthen me during life, defend me at the hour of death, and lead me to life everlasting.

LITANIES

Litany of the Sacred Heart of Jesus

Lord, have mercy on us.
 Lord, have mercy on us.
Christ, have mercy on us.
 Christ, have mercy on us.
Lord, have mercy on us.
 Lord, have mercy on us.
Christ, hear us.
 Christ, graciously hear us.
God the Father of heaven
 after each invocation: have mercy on us.
God the Son, Redeemer of the world
God the Holy Spirit
Holy Trinity, one God
Heart of Jesus, Son of the Eternal Father
Heart of Jesus, formed by the Holy Spirit in the womb of the Virgin Mother
Heart of Jesus, hypostatically united to the Eternal Word
Heart of Jesus, of infinite majesty
Heart of Jesus, holy temple of God
Heart of Jesus, tabernacle of the Most High
Heart of Jesus, house of God and gate of heaven
Heart of Jesus, burning furnace of charity
Heart of Jesus, vessel of justice and love
Heart of Jesus, full of goodness and love
Heart of Jesus, abyss of all virtues

Heart of Jesus, worthy of all praise
Heart of Jesus, king and centre of all hearts
Heart of Jesus, in which are all the treasures of wisdom and knowledge
Heart of Jesus, in which dwells all the fullness of the divinity
Heart of Jesus, in which the Father is well pleased
Heart of Jesus, of whose fullness we have all received
Heart of Jesus, desire of eternal hills
Heart of Jesus, patient and abounding in mercy
Heart of Jesus, rich unto all that call upon you
Heart of Jesus, fountain of life and holiness
Heart of Jesus, the propitiation for our sins
Heart of Jesus, filled with reproaches
Heart of Jesus, bruised for our sins
Heart of Jesus, made obedient unto death
Heart of Jesus, pierced with a lance
Heart of Jesus, source of all consolation
Heart of Jesus, our life and resurrection
Heart of Jesus, our peace and reconciliation
Heart of Jesus, victim for our sins
Heart of Jesus, salvation of those who hope in you
Heart of Jesus, hope of those who die in you
Heart of Jesus, delight of all the saints
Lamb of God, you take away the sins of the world
spare us, O Lord.

Lamb of God, you take away the sins of
  the world,
    graciously hear us, O Lord.
Lamb of God, you take away the sins of
  the world,
    have mercy on us.
Jesus, meek and humble of heart,
  make our hearts like unto yours.

Let us pray. Almighty and eternal God, consider the Heart of your well-beloved Son and the praises and satisfaction he offers you in the name of sinners; appeased by worthy homage, pardon those who implore your mercy, in the name of the same Jesus Christ your Son who lives and reigns with you and the Holy Spirit, one God, for ever and ever. Amen.

Litany of the Most Holy Name of Jesus

Lord, have mercy on us.
  Lord, have mercy on us.
Christ, have mercy on us.
  Christ, have mercy on us.
Lord, have mercy on us.
  Lord, have mercy on us.
Jesus, hear us.
  Jesus, graciously hear us.
God the Father of heaven
  after each invocation: have mercy on us.
God the Son, Redeemer of the world

God the Holy Spirit
Holy Trinity, one God
Jesus, Son of the living God
Jesus, splendour of the Father
Jesus, brightness of eternal light
Jesus, king of glory
Jesus, sun of justice
Jesus, Son of the Virgin Mary
Jesus most amiable
Jesus most admirable
Jesus, mighty God
Jesus, angel of great counsel
Jesus most powerful
Jesus most patient
Jesus most obedient
Jesus, meek and humble of heart
Jesus, lover of chastity
Jesus, lover of us
Jesus, God of peace
Jesus, author of life
Jesus, example of virtues
Jesus, zealous for souls
Jesus, our God
Jesus, our refuge
Jesus, father of the poor
Jesus, treasure of the faithful
Jesus, good shepherd
Jesus, true light
Jesus, eternal wisdom
Jesus, infinite goodness
Jesus, our way and our life

Jesus, joy of angels
Jesus, king of patriarchs
Jesus, master of the apostles
Jesus, teacher of the evangelists
Jesus, strength of martyrs
Jesus, light of confessors
Jesus, purity of virgins
Jesus, crown of all saints

Be merciful unto us,
    Jesus, spare us.
Be merciful unto us,
    Jesus, spare us.
From all evil
    after each invocation: Jesus, deliver us.
From all sin
From your wrath
From the snares of the devil
From the spirit of uncleanness
From everlasting death
From the neglect of your inspirations
Through the mystery of your holy Incarnation
Through your nativity
Through your infancy
Through your most divine life
Through your labours
Through your agony and passion
Through your cross and dereliction
Through your faintness and weariness
Through your death and burial
Through your resurrection

Through your ascension
Through your institution of the Most Holy
 Eucharist
Through your joys
Through your glory
Lamb of God, you take away the sins of
 the world,
 spare us, O Jesus.
Lamb of God, you take away the sins of
 the world,
 graciously, hear us, O Jesus.
Lamb of God, you take away the sins of
 the world,
 have mercy on us, O Jesus.
Jesus hear us,
 Jesus, graciously hear us.

Let us pray. O Lord Jesus Christ, who said, 'Ask and you shall receive, seek and you shall find, knock and it shall be opened unto you'; grant, we beseech you, to us your supplicants, the gifts of your most divine love, that we may love you with our whole heart, and in all our words and works, and never cease from praising you.

O Lord, give us a perpetual fear as well as love of your holy Name, for you never cease to govern those you founded upon the strength of your love. You who live live and reign for ever and ever. Amen.

Litany of Our Lady

Lord, have mercy on us.
>Lord, have mercy on us.

Christ, have mercy on us.
>Christ, have mercy on us.

Lord, have mercy on us.
>Lord, have mercy on us.

Christ, hear us.
>Christ, graciously hear us.

God the Father of heaven,
>have mercy on us.

God the Son, Redeemer of the world,
>have mercy on us.

God the Holy Spirit,
>have mercy on us.

Holy Trinity, one God,
>have mercy on us.

Holy Mary
>*after each invocation:* pray for us.

Holy Mother of God
Holy Virgin of virgins
Mother of Christ
Mother of divine grace
Mother most pure
Mother most chaste
Mother inviolate
Mother undefiled
Mother most lovable
Mother most admirable
Mother of good counsel

Mother of our Creator
Mother of our Redeemer
Virgin most prudent
Virgin most venerable
Virgin most renowned
Virgin most powerful
Virgin most merciful
Virgin most faithful
Mirror of justice
Seat of wisdom
Cause of our joy
Spiritual vessel
Vessel of honour
Singular vessel of devotion
Mystical rose
Tower of David
Tower of ivory
House of gold
Ark of the covenant
Gate of heaven
Morning star
Health of the sick
Refuge of sinners
Comforter of the afflicted
Help of Christians
Queen of angels
Queen of patriarchs
Queen of prophets
Queen of apostles
Queen of martyrs
Queen of confessors

Queen of virgins
Queen of all saints
Queen conceived without original sin
Queen assumed into heaven
Queen of the most holy rosary
Queen of peace
Lamb of God, you take away the sins of the world,
 spare us, O Lord.
Lamb of God, you take away the sins of the world,
 graciously hear us, O Lord.
Lamb of God, you take away the sins of the world,
 have mercy on us.
Pray for us, O holy Mother of God,
that we may be made worthy of the promises of Christ.

Let us pray. Grant that we your servants, Lord, may enjoy unfailing health of mind and body, and through the prayers of the ever blessed Virgin Mary in her glory, free us from our sorrows in this world and give us eternal happiness in the next. Through Christ our Lord. Amen.

Litany of Saints

Names of saints may be added, especially local and patron saints.

Lord, have mercy on us.
>Lord, have mercy on us.

Christ, have mercy on us.
>Christ, have mercy on us.

Lord, have mercy on us.
>Lord, have mercy on us.

Christ, hear us.
Jesus, graciously hear us.
Holy Mary, Mother of God
>*after each invocation*: pray for us.

Saint Michael
Saint Gabriel
Saint Raphael
Holy angels of God
Saint John the Baptist
Saint Joseph
Saint Peter and Saint Paul
Saint Andrew
Saint James
Saint John
Saint Thomas
Saint James
Saint Philip
Saint Bartholomew
Saint Matthew
Saint Simon
Saint Jude
Saint Matthias

Saint Luke
Saint Mark
Saint Stephen
Saint Mary Magdalene
Saint Ignatius
Saint Lawrence
Saint Vincent
Saint Fabian and Saint Sebastian
Saint Cosmas and Saint Damian
Saint Sylvester
Saint Gregory
Saint Ambrose
Saint Augustine
Saint Jerome
Saint Athanasius
Saint Basil
Saint Martin
Saint Nicholas
Saint Anthony
Saint Benedict
Saint Francis
Saint Dominic
Saint Perpetua and Saint Felicity
Saint Agatha
Saint Lucy
Saint Agnes
Saint Cecilia
Saint Anastasia
Saint Catherine
Saint Teresa of Avila
Saint Therese of the Child Jesus
Saint Francis Xavier

Saint John Vianney
Saint Patrick
Saint Columba
Saint Brigid
Saint Thomas Becket
Saint John Fisher
Saint Thomas More
Saint John Ogilvie
All holy men and women
Lord, be merciful
    Lord, save your people.
From all evil
    Lord, save your people.
From every sin
    Lord, save your people.
From everlasting death
    Lord, save your people.
By your coming as man
    Lord, save your people.
By your death and rising to new life
    Lord, save your people.
By your gift of the Holy Spirit
    Lord, save your people.
Be merciful to us sinners
    Lord, hear our prayer.
Jesus, Son of the living God
    Lord, hear our prayer.
Christ, hear us
    Christ, hear us.
Lord Jesus, hear our prayer
    Lord Jesus, hear our prayer.

THE ROSARY

This vocal and meditative form of prayer, which is now an integral part of Catholic devotional practice, was begun by a Dominican preacher, Alan de Rupe, in the fifteenth century. The devotion is directed to the Blessed Virgin Mary. It consists of an initial prayer, the Apostles' Creed, followed by the Our Father, three Hail Marys and a Glory be to the Father. We are then led step by step through the essential facts, traditionally known as mysteries, of our faith. There are fifteen such mysteries in the rosary, and they are arranged in groups of five decades (also known as chaplets) that follow the historical sequence of the life of Jesus and his Blessed Mother Mary. We meditate on the main event or mystery of each decade as we recite one Our Father, ten Hail Marys and one Glory be to the Father. It is customary to recite only one group of five of the fifteen decades which are divided into joyful, sorrowful and glorious mysteries.

The Joyful Mysteries

1. The Annunciation

In the first joyful mystery we contemplate the annunciation by the angel Gabriel to the Blessed Virgin Mary that she would conceive Jesus our Saviour by the Holy Spirit.

Reading: Luke 1:26-38

'Here I am, the servant of the Lord;
let it be with me according to your word.'

Lord Jesus,
open our hearts to the Holy Spirit
and make your home in us.

2. The Visitation

In the second joyful mystery we contemplate the visitation of Our Lady to Elizabeth, the mother of John the Baptist who would announce the public ministry of Jesus.

Reading: Luke 1:39-56

'Blessed are you among women,
and blessed is the fruit of your womb!'

Lord Jesus,
give us the spirit of generosity
that we may serve you
unreservedly in others.

3. The Birth of Jesus

In the third joyful mystery we contemplate the birth of Jesus in a stable in Bethlehem, where shepherds came to worship him.

Reading: Luke 2:1-21

She gave birth to her firstborn son
and wrapped him in bands of cloth,
and laid him in a manger.

Lord Jesus,
be born again in me today,
and help me to see you in the world
and in all human beings.

4. The Presentation

In the fourth joyful mystery we contemplate the presentation of the child Jesus in the Temple in Jerusalem, where Simeon the prophet was led by the Holy Spirit to recognize the child whom he took into his arms and praised God.

Reading: Luke 2:22-40

'My eyes have seen your salvation
which you have prepared
in the presence of all peoples.'

Lord Jesus,
let me first be pruned
so that I may bear fruit
and witness to the salvation
you have brought to the world.

5. The Finding in the Temple

In the fifth joyful mystery we contemplate the finding of the boy Jesus in the Temple, sitting among the doctors and discussing with them.

Reading: Luke 2:41-52

'Why were you searching for me?
Did you not know
that I must be in my Father's house?'

Lord Jesus,
grant me the grace
to imitate you in placing
your Father's kingdom first.

THE SORROWFUL MYSTERIES

1. The Agony in the garden

In the first sorrowful mystery we contemplate the agony of Jesus in the garden of Gethsemane, where his sweat became like drops of blood.

Reading: Luke 22:39-46

'Father, if you are willing,
remove this cup from me;
yet, not my will but yours be done.'

Lord Jesus,
in all our trials and sufferings,
teach us to pray
that God's will may be done.

2. The Scourging at the pillar

In the second sorrowful mystery we contemplate the scourging of Jesus at the pillar by the order of Pontius Pilate, who washed his hands in public before handing Jesus over to be crucified.

Reading: Matthew 27:21-26

'What should I do with Jesus who is called the Messiah? Why, what evil has he done?'

Lord Jesus,
present in all those who suffer,
give me the strength to heal broken hearts.

3. The Crowning with thorns

In the third sorrowful mystery we contemplate the crowning of Jesus with thorns and his humiliation at the hands of the soldiers.

Reading: Matthew 27:27-31

They stripped him
and put a scarlet robe on him,
and after twisting some thorns into a crown,
they put it on his head.

Lord Jesus,
help me to remove a thorn where I can
and to plant a flower in its place.

4. The Carrying of the cross

In the fourth sorrowful mystery we contemplate the carrying of the cross by Jesus, who is helped on the way by Simon of Cyrene.

Reading: Luke 23:26-31

As they led him away,
they seized a man, Simon of Cyrene,
and laid the cross on him,
and made him carry it behind Jesus.

Lord Jesus,
give me strength
to deny myself and take up my cross,
and follow you.

5. The Crucifixion

In the fifth sorrowful mystery we contemplate the crucifixion of Jesus on Calvary where, hanging on the cross, he forgave his enemies and promised paradise to the good thief before surrendering his spirit to the Father.

Reading: Luke 23:33-49

'Father,
into your hands I commend my spirit.'

Lord Jesus,
teach me self-abandonment
to your Father's love.

The Glorious Mysteries

1. The Resurrection

In the first glorious mystery we contemplate the resurrection of Jesus on the third day as he had foretold.

Reading: Luke 24:1-12

'Why do you look for the living among the dead? He is not here; but has risen.'

Lord Jesus,
let me be reminded of your resurrection
in every act of
forgiveness, trust, friendship,
and in our faith
which would otherwise be vain.

2. The Ascension

In the second glorious mystery we contemplate the ascension of Jesus into heaven, whence he will come again to judge the living and the dead.

Reading: Mark 16:14-20

'Go into all the world and proclaim the good news to the whole creation.'

Lord Jesus,
help me to be a witness
to the good news of your kingdom

by proclaiming your word
and by loving you
and my fellow beings.

3. The Coming of the Holy Spirit

In the third glorious mystery we contemplate the coming of the Holy Spirit, who guides us in truth and wisdom.

Reading: John 14:15-26

'The Holy Spirit,
whom the Father will send in my name,
will remind you of all that I have said to you.'

Come, O Holy Spirit,
and kindle in us
the fire of your love.

4. The Assumption of the Blessed Virgin Mary

In the fourth glorious mystery we contemplate the assumption of the Blessed Virgin Mary, who was taken to heaven body and soul.

Reading: Revelation 12:1-17

A great portent appeared in heaven:
a woman clothed with the sun,
with the moon under her feet,
and on her head a crown of twelve stars.

Mother of Jesus,
pray for us sinners,
now and at the hour of our death.

5. The Coronation of Mary and the joy of all in heaven

In the fifth glorious mystery we contemplate the coronation of the Blessed Virgin Mary and the joy of all those who are in heaven.

Reading: Luke 1:46-55

'All generations will call me blessed;
for the One has done great things for me,
and holy is his name.'

Mary, my Mother,
pray for me that I may
one day share in your joy
and see the Father in all his glory.

BENEDICTION

Benediction is a devotion to Christ present in the Eucharist. It consists of the exposition of the Blessed Sacrament in the monstrance, adoration by the faithful through prayers, hymns, readings from the Scriptures, silence, and the blessing where the priest makes the sign of the cross over the people with the Blessed Sacrament. It ends with an acclamation.

O salutaris hostia,
quae coeli pandis ostium;
bella premunt hostilia,
da robur, fer auxilium.
Uni Trinoque Domino
sit sempiterna gloria,
qui vitam sine termino
nobis donet in patria. Amen.

***

O saving victim, opening wide
the gate of heaven to man below;
our foes press on from every side;
your aid supply, your strength bestow.

To your great name be endless praise,
immortal Godhead, one in three;
O grant us endless length of days
in our true native land with thee. Amen.

✦

Tantum ergo Sacramentum
veneremur cernui:
et antiquum documentum
novo cedat ritui:
praestet fides supplementum
sensuum defectui.

Genitori Genitoque
laus et iubilatio.
Salus, honor, virtus quoque
sit et benedictio;
Procedenti ab utroque
compar sit laudatio. Amen.

***

Come, adore this wondrous presence,
bow to Christ, the source of grace.
Here is kept the ancient promise
of Gods earthly dwelling-place.
Sight is blind before Gods glory,
faith alone may see his face.

Glory be to God the Father,
praise to his co-equal Son,
adoration to the Spirit,
bond of love, in Godhead one.
Blest be God by all creation
joyously while ages run. Amen

T. James Quinn

Oremus. Deus, qui nobis, sub sacramento mirabili, passionis tuae memoriam reliquisti: tribue quaesumus, ita nos Corporis et Sanguinis tui sacra mysteria venerari, ut redemptionis tuae fructum in nobis jugiter sentiamus: qui vivis et regnas in saecula saeculorum. Amen.

***

Let us pray. O God, who in this wonderful sacrament has left us a memorial of your passion: help us to reverence the sacred mysteries of your Body and Blood, that we may experience in our lives the effects of your redemption: who live and reign for ever and ever. Amen.

♦

Blessed be God.
Blessed be his holy Name.
Blessed be Jesus Christ true God and true man.
Blessed be the name of Jesus.
Blessed be his most Sacred Heart.
Blessed be his most Precious Blood.
Blessed be Jesus in the most holy Sacrament of the altar.
Blessed be the Holy Spirit, the Paraclete.
Blessed be the great Mother of God, Mary most holy.
Blessed be her holy and Immaculate Conception.

Blessed be her glorious Assumption.
Blessed be the name of Mary, Virgin
and Mother.
Blessed be Saint Joseph, her spouse most chaste.
Blessed be God in his angels and in his saints.

◆

Adoremus in aeternum sanctissimum
sacramentum.

Laudate Dominum omnes gentes;
laudate eum omnes populi.

Quoniam confirmata est super misericordia eius:
et veritas Domini manet in aeternum.

Gloria Patri, et Filio,
et Spiritui Sancto.

Sicut erat in principio, et nunc et semper,
et in saecula saeculorum. Amen.

THE STATIONS OF THE CROSS

In the Stations of the Cross, which is an expression of our devotion to the passion of Christ, we trace the footsteps of the Lord as he carried his cross from Pilate's house to Golgotha, the place of the crucifixion. The devotion is believed to have originated with the crusaders, and those unable to make a journey to Jerusalem. The stations, also known as the Way of the Cross, were set up in churches throughout Europe. In the sixteenth century fourteen stations were fixed and approved by the Church, but today it has become customary to add another station to denote the resurrection of Jesus from the dead. The fifteenth station gives expression to the prominence of the resurrection which has come to permeate our thinking on suffering and death.

The stations may be made alone or in a group. The chosen text may be omitted if one prefers to pause before each station in private prayer and meditation.

First Station

Jesus is condemned to death

We adore you, O Christ, and we bless you.
Because by your holy cross you have redeemed the world.

After being scourged and crowned with thorns, Jesus is unjustly condemned by Pilate to die on the cross. Are we just or unjust in our dealings?

Reading: John 19:4-16

Lord Jesus,
if I have to judge
let me do so with justice,
mercy and selflessness.

Lord, by your cross and resurrection
you have set us free.
You are the Saviour of the world.

Second Station

Jesus takes up his cross

We adore you, O Christ, and we bless you.
Because by your holy cross you have redeemed the world.

Jesus carries the cross on his shoulders and offers his Father the death he is about to undergo for our salvation. We are called to take up our cross daily.

Reading: Matthew 11:29-30

Lord Jesus,
I wish to take up
my cross with you daily.
Help me to bear patiently
whatever comes my way.

Lord, by your cross and resurrection
you have set us free.
You are the Saviour of the world.

Third Station

Jesus falls the first time

We adore you, O Christ, and we bless you.
Because by your holy cross you have redeemed the world.

Jesus' flesh is torn by the scourging, his head is crowned with thorns, and he can scarcely walk. Yet he has to carry the cross. Let us not be discouraged at the first sign of failure in our Christian life.

Reading: Isaiah 53:6-12

Lord Jesus,
may the suffering you endured
restore hope to a fallen world,
bringing healing and comfort
to those who suffer.

Lord, by your cross and resurrection
you have set us free.
You are the Saviour of the world.

Fourth Station

Jesus meets his mother

We adore you, O Christ, and we bless you.
Because by your holy cross you have redeemed the world.

Jesus, bearing the cross, sees his mother, whose soul is pierced by a sword of sorrow. The hearts of Jesus and Mary are united in the same suffering. Let us ask for the grace to face life's trials like Jesus and Mary.

Reading: Luke 2:22-35

Lord Jesus,
you willed that your mother
should be with you
on your way to Calvary:
give me an undaunted spirit
to face life's trials
as Mary your mother did.

Lord, by your cross and resurrection
you have set us free.
You are the Saviour of the world.

Fifth Station

Simon of Cyrene
helps Jesus to carry his cross

We adore you, O Christ, and we bless you.
Because by your holy cross you have redeemed the world.

The executioners of Jesus force a man from the crowd to carry the cross of Jesus. We are also called to cooperate in the redemption of the world by completing with our sufferings the passion of Jesus Christ.

Reading: Isaiah 52:14

Lord Jesus,
give me a generous heart
to accept my duties and responsibilities
even when they seem
too heavy to bear.

Lord, by your cross and resurrection
you have set us free.
You are the Saviour of the world.

Sixth Station

Veronica wipes the face of Jesus

We adore you, O Christ, and we bless you.
Because by your holy cross you have redeemed the world.

The holy woman Veronica sees Jesus bathed in sweat and blood; and she wipes his face with a towel. Jesus rewards her by leaving the impression of his face on her towel. May we see the face of Jesus in the poor and the suffering.

Reading: Isaiah 53:2-5

Lord Jesus,
imprint on me your virtues of
compassion, kindness, love,
meekness, patience and forgiveness.

Lord, by your cross and resurrection
you have set us free.
You are the Saviour of the world.

Seventh Station

Jesus falls the second time

We adore you, O Christ, and we bless you.
Because by your holy cross you have redeemed the world.

Under the heavy burden of his cross, Jesus falls a second time. This is a reminder to us that we should not take Jesus' perseverance for granted: he was human like us in everything except sin.

Reading: Hebrews 5:7-10

Lord Jesus,
when all my efforts seem to fail,
help me to trust in your help.

Lord, by your cross and resurrection
you have set us free.
You are the Saviour of the world.

Eighth Station

The women of Jerusalem mourn for Jesus

We adore you, O Christ, and we bless you.
Because by your holy cross you have redeemed the world.

Seeing Jesus in such a pitiable state, the women of Jerusalem weep for him. But Jesus tells them, 'Daughters of Jerusalem, do not weep for me, but for yourselves and your children.' May we be mindful of the sufferings of others.

Reading: Luke 23:27-32

Lord Jesus,
you found the strength
to console the women of Jerusalem
despite your own sufferings;
give me strength
to bring comfort
to those in sorrow.

Lord, by your cross and resurrection
you have set us free.
You are the Saviour of the world.

Ninth Station

Jesus falls the third time

We adore you, O Christ, and we bless you.
Because by your holy cross you have redeemed the world.

Jesus grows weaker, but the executioners hurry him. And Jesus falls for a third time. Whenever we fall, let us not lose heart, but renew our faith in the power of Christ.

Reading: Romans 7:15-25

Lord Jesus,
when anxiety and fear
cause me to lose heart,
give me support
that I may walk steadily
in your way.

Lord, by your cross and resurrection
you have set us free.
You are the Saviour of the world.

Tenth Station

Jesus is stripped of his clothes

We adore you, O Christ, and we bless you.
Because by your holy cross you have redeemed the world.

Jesus is stripped by those who have charge of crucifying him. If we want to be poor in spirit like Jesus, then we should ask ourselves why we are sometimes so concerned about trivialities.

Reading: John 19:2-24

Lord Jesus,
grant me the grace
to detach my heart
from all sinful vanities,
so that I may seek only you,
my supreme and eternal happiness.

Lord, by your cross and resurrection
you have set us free.
You are the Saviour of the world.

Eleventh Station

Jesus is nailed to the cross

We adore you, O Christ, and we bless you.
Because by your holy cross you have redeemed the world.

Stretched out on the cross, Jesus' body is racked by pain. Yet he yields his hands and feet to be nailed to the cross in ransom for the salvation of humanity. Let us reflect upon the part we may be playing in perpetuating cruelty today.

Reading: Luke 23:33-43

Lord Jesus,
help me to heal the wounds
caused by hate
and to witness to your love
that did not count the cost.

Lord, by your cross and resurrection
you have set us free.
You are the Saviour of the world.

Twelfth Station

Jesus dies on the cross

We adore you, O Christ, and we bless you.
Because by your holy cross you have redeemed the world.

After suffering anguish and pain for three hours on the cross, Jesus commends his spirit to the Father and dies. Let us meditate on the mystery of love through which the sacrifice on Calvary is repeated in the Eucharistic celebration.

Reading: Luke 24:44-49

Lord Jesus,
your death brought
life into the world.
Grant that my life
may be a source of joy
to those whose paths cross mine.

Lord, by your cross and resurrection
you have set us free.
You are the Saviour of the world.

Thirteenth Station

Jesus is taken down from the cross

We adore you, O Christ, and we bless you.
Because by your holy cross you have redeemed the world.

After Jesus' death, two of his disciples, Joseph and Nicodemus, took him down from the cross and placed him in the arms of his sorrowful mother. May we be free from sin when we leave this world and rejoice with Christ.

Reading: Matthew 27:55-58

Lord Jesus,
help me to approach death
unafraid,
confident that I have tried
to do your will.

Lord, by your cross and resurrection
you have set us free.
You are the Saviour of the world.

Fourteenth Station

Jesus is placed in the tomb

We adore you, O Christ, and we bless you.
Because by your holy cross you have redeemed the world.

The disciples anoint the body of Jesus and place it in the tomb. They roll a huge stone and seal the entrance. We must draw comfort from the fact that the grave is only a passing resting place for us as it was for Jesus.

Reading: Mark 15:42-47

Lord Jesus,
give us strength to endure
our daily frustrations and sufferings,
and make us understand
that you give meaning
even to our death.

Lord, by your cross and resurrection
you have set us free.
You are the Saviour of the world.

Fifteenth Station

Jesus is risen

We adore you, O Christ, and we bless you.
Because by your holy cross you have redeemed the world.

Jesus rises from the dead in the glory of the resurrection. We have been raised to life with Christ; let us set our hearts on the things that are in heaven.

Reading: Jn 20:11-18

Lord Jesus,
give me the hope
and the joy
of spending eternity with you.

Lord, by your cross and resurrection
you have set us free.
You are the Saviour of the world.

PRAYERS FROM THE BIBLE

The Lord is my strength and my song,
 and he has become my salvation;
this is my God, and I will praise him,
 my father's God, and I will exalt him.

Exodus 15:2

◆

Have regard to the prayer of thy servant and to his supplication, O Lord my God, hearkening to the cry and to the prayer which thy servant prays before thee this day; that thy eyes may be open night and day toward this house. Hear thou in heaven thy dwelling place; and when thou hearest, forgive.

1 Kings 8:28-30

◆

Blessed are you, O Lord, the God of our ancestor Israel, for ever and ever.

Yours, O Lord, are the greatness, the power, the glory, the victory, and the majesty; for all that is in the heavens and on the earth is yours; yours is the kingdom, O Lord, and you are exalted as head above all. Riches and honour come from you, and you rule over all. In your hand are power and might; and it is in your hand to make great and to give strength to all. And now, our God, we give thanks to you and praise your glorious name.

1 Chronicles 29:10-13

✦

Save us by your hand, and help me, who am alone and have no helper but you, O Lord. O God, whose might is over all, hear the voice of the despairing, and save us from the hands of evildoers. And save me from my fear!

Esther 14:14.19

✦

O Lord God of heaven, the great and awesome God who keeps covenant and steadfast love with those who love him and keep his commandments. We have offended you deeply, failing to keep your commandments. Let your ear be attentive and your eyes open to hear the prayer of your servant that I now pray before you night and day for your servants. They are your servants and your people, whom you redeemed by your great power and strong hand. O Lord, let your ear be attentive to the prayer of your servants who delight in revering your name.

Nehemiah 1:5-7.11

✦

O Lord, you are our Father;
>we are the clay, and you are our potter;
>we are all the work of your hand.

Isaiah 64:8

♦

Heal me, O Lord, and I shall be healed;
>save me, and I shall be saved;
>for you are my praise.

Jeremiah 17:14

♦

You have rescued me in time of trouble.
For this reason I thank you and praise you,
>and I bless the name of the Lord.

Sirach 51:12

♦

But you, O Lord, reign for ever;
>your throne endures for all generations.
Why have you forgotten us completely?
>Why have you forsaken us these many days?
Restore us to yourself, O Lord,
>that we may be restored.

Lamentations 5:19-21

♦

Blessed are you, O Lord, God of our ancestors,
    and to be praised and highly exalted forever;
And blessed is your glorious, holy name,
    and to be higly praised and highly exalted
        forever;
Blessed are you in the temple of your holy glory,
    and to be extolled and highly glorified
        forever.
Bless the Lord, you heavens;
    sing praise to him and highly
        exalt him forever.
Bless the Lord, nights and days;
    sing praise to him and highly
        exalt him forever.
Let the earth bless the Lord;
    let it sing praise to him and
        highly exalt him forever.
Bless the Lord, all wild animals and cattle
    sing praise to him and highly
        exalt him forever.
Bless the Lord, all people on earth;
    sing praise to him and highly
        exalt him forever.
Give thanks to the Lord, for he is good,
    for his mercy endures for ever.

Prayer of Azariah 29ff

◆

But you, our God, are kind and true,
    patient, and ruling all things in mercy.

For even if we sin we are yours,
  knowing your power;
but we will not sin, because we
  know that you
  acknowledge us as yours.
For to know you is complete
  righteousness,
and to know your power is the
  root of immortality.

Wisdom 15:1-3

◆

Have mercy on me, O God,
  according to your steadfast love;
according to your abundant mercy
  blot out my transgressions.
Wash me thoroughly from my iniquity,
  and cleanse me from my sin.
For I know my transgresions,
  and my sin is always before me.
Against you, you alone, have I sinned,
  and done what is evil in your sight.
Purge me with hyssop, and I shall be clean;
  wash me, and I shall be whiter than snow.
Hide your face from my sins,
  and blot out all my iniquities.
Create in me a clean heart, O God,
  and put a new and right spirit within me.
Do not cast me away from your presence,

and do not take your holy spirit from me.
Restore to me the joy of your salvation,
    and sustain in me a willing spirit.

Psalm 51:1-3.4.7.9-12

◆

Out of the depths I cry to you, O Lord.
    Lord, hear my voice!
Let your ears be attentive
    to the voice of my supplications!
If you, O Lord, should mark our iniquities,
    Lord, who could stand?
But there is forgiveness with you:
    so that you may be revered.

I wait for the Lord, my soul waits,
    and in his word I hope;
my soul waits for the Lord
    more than those who watch for the morning,
    more than those who watch for the morning.

O Israel, hope in the Lord!
    For with the Lord there is steadfast love,
    and with him is great power to redeem.
It is he who will redeem Israel
    from all its iniquities.

Psalm 130

◆

Praise the Lord, all you nations!
    Extol him, all you peoples!

For great is his steadfast love toward us,
> and the faithfulness of the Lord
>> endures forever.
Praise the Lord!

Psalm 117

✦

I have sinned, O Lord,
> I have sinned,
> and I acknowledge my transgressions.
I earnestly implore you,
> forgive me, O Lord, forgive me!
Do not destroy me with my transgressions!
Do not be angry with me forever
> or store up evil for me;
do not condemn me to the depths
> of the earth.
For you, O Lord, are the God
> of those who repent.

Prayer of Manasseh 12-13

✦

My soul magnifies the Lord,
> and my spirit rejoices in God my Saviour,
for he has looked with favour on the
> lowliness of his servant.
> Surely, from now on all generations
>> will call me blessed;

for the Mighty One has done
> great things for me,
> and holy is his name.

His mercy is for those who fear him
> from generation to generation.

He has shown strength with his arm;
> he has scattered the proud in the
> > thoughts of their hearts.

He has brought down the powerful from
> their thrones,
> and lifted up the lowly;

he has filled the hungry with good things,
> and sent the rich away empty.

He has helped his servant Israel,
> in remembrance of his mercy,

according to the promise he made to
> our ancestors,
> to Abraham and to his descendants forever.

Luke 1:47-55

✦

This is eternal life,
that they may know you,
the only true God,
and Jesus Christ
whom you have sent.
Sanctify them in the truth;
your word is truth.

John 17:3.17

Blessed be the God and Father of our Lord Jesus Christ, the Father of mercies and the God of all consolation, who consoles us in all our affliction with the consolation with which we ourselves are consoled by God.

2 Corinthians 1:3-4

♦

You are worthy, our Lord and God,
to receive glory and honour and power,
for you created all things.
and by your will they existed
    and were created.
Worthy is the Lamb that was slaughtered
to receive power and wealth and
    wisdom and might
and honour and glory and blessing!

Revelation 4:11; 5:12

See also: page 7: *Our Father* (Matthew 6:9-13); page 7: *Hail Mary* (cf Luke 1:26-45).

HYMNS

To God the Father

All people that on earth do dwell,
   sing to the Lord with cheerful voice;
him serve with fear, his praise forth tell,
   come ye before him and rejoice.

The Lord, ye know, is God indeed,
   without our aid he did us make;
we are his folk he doth us feed
   and for his sheep he doth us take.

O enter then his gates with praise,
   approach with joy his courts unto;
praise, laud and bless his name always,
   for it is seemly so to do.

For why the Lord our God is good:
   his mercy is for ever sure;
his truth at all times firmly stood,
   and shall from age to age endure.

To Father, Son and Holy Ghost,
   the God whom heaven and earth adore,
from men and from the angel-host
   be praise and glory evermore.

William Kethe, based on Psalm 100

Amazing grace! How sweet the sound
    that saved a wretch like me.
I once was lost, but now I'm found,
    was blind, but now I see.

'Twas grace that taught my heart to fear,
    and grace my fears relieved.
How precious did that grace appear
    the hour I first believed.

Through many dangers, toils and snares
    I have already come.
'Tis grace hath brought me safe thus far,
    and grace will lead me home.

The Lord has promised good to me;
    his word my hope secures.
He will my shield and portion be
    as long as life endures.

John Newton (1725-1807)

◆

God be with you till we meet again!
By his counsels guide, uphold you,
with his sheep securely fold you;
God be with you till we meet again.

Till we meet! till we meet!
Till we meet at Jesus' feet;
Till we meet! Till we meet!
God be with you till we meet again.

God be with you till we meet again!
Neath his wing securely hid you,
daily manna still provide you;
God be with you till we meet again!

God be with you till we meet again!
Keep love's banner floating o'er you,
smite death's threat'ning wave before you;
God be with you till we meet again!

Jeremiah Rankin

✦

God of mercy and compassion,
    look with pity upon me;
Father, let me call thee Father,
    'tis thy child returns to thee.

Jesus Lord, I ask for mercy;
    let me not implore in vain:
all my sins I now detest them,
    never will I sin again.

See our Saviour, bleeding, dying,
    on the cross of Calvary;
to that cross my sins have nail'd him,
    yet he bleeds and dies for me.

E. Vaughan (1827-1908)

✦

Now thank we all our God,
with heart and hands and voices,
who wondrous things hath done,
in whom this world rejoices;
who from our mother's arms
hath blessed us on our way
with countless gifts of love,
and still is ours today.

O may this bounteous God
through all our life be near us,
with ever joyful hearts
and blessed peace to cheer us;
and keep us in his grace,
and guide us when perplexed,
and free us from all ills
in this world and the next.

All praise and thanks to God
the Father now be given,
the Son and him who reigns
with them in highest heaven,
the one eternal God,
whom earth and heaven adore;
for thus it was, is now,
and shall be evermore.

Martin Rinkart (1586-1649)
tr. Catherine Winkworth

Praise, my soul, the king of heaven!
  To his feet thy tribute bring.
Ransomed, healed, restored, forgiven,
  who like me his praise should sing?
Praise him! Praise him! (twice)
Praise the everlasting king!

Praise him for his grace and favour
  to our fathers in distress;
praise him still the same for ever,
  slow to chide and swift to bless.
Praise him! Praise him! (twice)
Glorious in his faithfulness!

Father-like he tends and spares us;
  well our feeble frame he knows:
in his hands he gently bears us,
  rescues us from all our foes.
Praise him! Praise him! (twice)
Widely as his mercy flows!

Angels, help us to adore him;
ye behold him face to face;
sun and moon bow down before him,
  dwellers all in time and space.
Praise him! Praise him! (twice)
Praise with us the God of grace!

Henry Francis Lyte (1793-1847)

Praise to the Holiest in the height,
    and in the depth be praise,
in all his words most wonderful,
    most sure in all his ways.

O loving wisdom of our God!
    When all was sin and shame,
a second Adam to the fight,
    and to the rescue came.

O wisest love! That flesh and blood
    which did in Adam fail,
should strive afresh against the foe,
    should strive and should prevail.

And that a higher gift than grace
    should flesh and blood refine,
God's presence and his very self,
    and essence all divine.

O generous love! that he who smote
    in man for man the foe,
the double agony in man
    for man should undergo.

And in the garden secretly
    and on the Cross on high,
should teach his brethren, and inspire
    to suffer and to die.

Praise to the Holiest in the height,
    and in the depth be praise,
in all his words most wonderful,
    most sure in all his ways.

John Henry Newman (1801-1890)

Praise to the Lord, the Almighty,
   the King of creation!
O my soul, praise him,
   for he is your health and salvation.
All you who hear,
   now to his altar draw near,
   join in profound adoration.

Praise to the Lord, let us offer
   our gifts at his altar;
let not our sins and transgressions
   now cause us to falter.
Christ, the High Priest,
   bids us all join in his feast;
   victims with him on the altar.

Praise to the Lord, oh, let all that
   is in us adore him!
All that has life and breath,
   come now in praises before him.
Let me Amen sound from
   his people again,
   now as we worship before him.

Joachim Neander (1650-1680)
tr. C. Winkworth

♦

Praise we our God with joy
and gladness never ending;
angels and saints with us
their grateful voices lending.

He is our Father dear,
o'er filled with parent's love;
mercies unsought, unknown,
he showers from above.

He is our shepherd true;
with watchful care unsleeping,
on us, his erring sheep
an eye of pity keeping;
he with a mighty arm
the bonds of sin doth break,
and to our burden'd hearts
in words of peace doth speak.

Graces in copious stream
from that pure fount are welling,
where, in our heart of hearts,
our God hath set his dwelling.
His word our lantern is;
his peace our comfort still;
his sweetness all our rest;
our law, our life, his will.

Frederick Oakeley (1802-1880)

◆

The Lord's my shepherd, I'll not want.
He makes me down to lie
in pastures green. He leadeth me
the quiet waters by.

My soul he doth restore again,
and me to walk doth make

within the paths of righteousness,
e'en for his own name's sake.

Yea, though I walk in death's dark vale,
yet will I fear none ill.
For thou art with me, and thy rod
and staff me comfort still.

My table thou hast furnishèd
in presence of my foes,
my head thou dost with oil anoint,
and my cup overflows.

Goodness and mercy all my life
shall surely follow me.
And in God's house for evermore
my dwelling place shall be.

*Paraphrased from Psalm 23
in the Scottish Psalter (1650)*

To Jesus

Abide with me, fast falls the eventide;
    the darkness deepens, Lord, with me abide!
When other helpers fail, and comforts flee,
    help of the helpless, O abide with me.

Swift to its close ebbs our life's little day;
    earth's joys grow dim, its glories pass away;
change and decay in all around I see;
    O thou who changest not, abide with me.

I need thy presence every passing hour;
  what but thy grace can foil the
    tempter's power?
Who like thyself my guide and stay can be?
  Through cloud and sunshine, O abide
    with me.

I fear no foe with thee at hand to bless;
  ills have no weight, and tears no bitterness.
Where is death's sting? Where, grave,
    thy victory?
  I triumph still if thou abide with me.

Hold thou thy Cross before my closing eyes;
  shine through the gloom, and point me to
    the skies;
heaven's morning breaks, and earth's vain
    shadows flee;
  in life, in death, O Lord, abide with me!

H.F. Lyte (1793-1847)

♦

Jesus, my Lord, my God, my all,
  how can I love thee as I ought?
And how revere this wondrous gift
  so far surpassing hope or thought?

  Sweet sacrament, we thee adore;
  Oh, make us love thee more and more.

Had I but Mary's sinless heart
    to love thee with, my dearest King,
Oh, with what bursts of fervent praise
    thy goodness, Jesus, would I sing!

Ah, see! within a creature's hand
    the vast Creator deigns to be,
reposing, infant-like, as though
    on Joseph's arm or Mary's knee.

Thy body, soul, and Godhead, all;
    O mystery of love divine!
I cannot compass all I have,
    for all thou hast and art are mine.

Sound, sound, his praises higher still,
    and come, ye angels, to our aid;
'tis God, 'tis God, the very God
    whose power both man and angels made.

Frederick William Faber (1814-1863)

◆

Soul of my Saviour, sanctify my breast;
Body of Christ, be thou my saving guest;
Blood of my Saviour, bathe me in thy tide,
wash me with waters flowing from thy side.

Strength and protection may thy passion be;
O Blessed Jesus, hear and answer me;
deep in thy wounds, Lord, hide and shelter me;
so shall I never, never part from thee.

Guard and defend me from the foe malign;
in death's dread moment make me only thine;
call me and bid me come to thee on high,
where I may praise thee with thy saints for aye.

Ascribed to John XXII (1249-1334)

◆

Sweet Heart of Jesus,
> fount of love and mercy,
today we come,
> thy blessing to implore;
O touch our hearts,
> so cold and so ungrateful,
and make them, Lord,
> thine own for evermore.

> Sweet Heart of Jesus, we implore,
> O make us love thee more and more.

Sweet Heart of Jesus,
> make us know and love thee,
unfold to us
> the treasures of thy grace;
that so our hearts,
> from things of earth uplifted,
may long alone
> to gaze upon thy face.

Sweet Heart of Jesus,
> make us pure and gentle,
and teach us how
> to do thy blessed will;

to follow close
    the print of thy dear footsteps,
and when we fall
    – Sweet Heart, oh, love us still.

Sweet Heart of Jesus,
    bless all hearts that love thee,
and may thine own
    Heart ever blessèd be;
bless us, dear Lord,
    and bless the friends we cherish,
and keep us true
    to Mary and to thee.

Author unknown

♦

To Jesus' Heart, all burning
    with fervent love for men,
my heart with fondest yearning
    shall raise its joyful strain.

    While ages course along,
        blest be with loudest song
    the Sacred Heart of Jesus
        by ev'ry heart and tongue.

O Heart, for men on fire
    with love no man can speak,
my yet untold desire
    God gives me for thy sake.

Too true, I have forsaken
 thy love for wilful sin;
yet now let me be taken
 back by thy grace again.

As thou art meek and lowly,
 and ever pure of heart,
so may my heart be wholly
 of thine the counterpart.

When life is flying,
 and earth's false glare is done:
still, Sacred Heart, in dying,
 I'll say I'm all thine own.

Aloys Schlor (1805-1852)
tr. A.J. Christie

♦

O bread of heaven, beneath this veil
 thou dost my very God conceal;
my Jesus, dearest treasure, hail;
 I love thee and adoring kneel;
each loving soul by thee is fed
 with thine own self in form of bread.

O food of life, thou who dost give
 the pledge of immortality;
I live; no, 'tis not I that live;
 God gives me life, God lives in me:
he feeds my soul, he guides my ways,
 and every grief with joy repays.

O bond of love, that dost unite
    the servant to his living Lord;
could I dare live, and not requite
    such love – then death were meet reward:
I cannot live unless to prove
    some love for such unmeasured love.

Beloved Lord in heaven above,
    there, Jesus, thou awaitest me;
to gaze on thee with changeless love,
    yes, thus I hope, thus shall it be:
for how can he deny me heaven
    who here on earth himself hath given?

St Alphonsus (1696-1787)
tr. E. Vaughan

◆

Sweet sacrament divine,
hid in thine earthly home,
lo! round thy lowly shrine,
with suppliant hearts we come;
Jesus, to thee our voice we raise,
in songs of love and heartfelt praise,
sweet sacrament divine.

Sweet sacrament of peace,
dear home of every heart,
where restless yearnings cease,
and sorrows all depart,
there in thine ear all trustfully
we tell our tale of misery,
sweet sacrament of peace.

Sweet sacrament of rest,
Ark from the ocean's roar,
within thy shelter blest
soon may we reach the shore;
save us, for still the tempest raves;
save, lest we sink beneath the waves,
sweet sacrament of rest.

Sweet sacrament divine,
earth's light and jubilee,
in thy far depths doth shine
thy Godhead's majesty;
sweet light, so shine on us, we pray,
that earthly joys may fade away,
sweet sacrament divine.

Francis Stanfield (1835-1914)

◆

Godhead here in hiding,
   whom I do adore,
masked by these bare shadows,
   shape and nothing more,
see, Lord, at thy service
   low lies here a heart
lost, all lost in wonder
   at the God thou art.

Seeing, touching, tasting
   are in thee deceived;
how says trusty hearing?
   that shall be believed;

what God's Son hath told me,
 take for truth I do;
truth himself speaks truly,
 or there's nothing true.

On the cross thy Godhead
 made no sign to men;
here thy very manhood
 steals from human ken;
both are my confession,
 both are my belief;
and I pray the prayer
 of the dying thief.

I am not like Thomas,
 wounds I cannot see,
but can plainly call thee
 Lord and God as he;
this faith each day deeper
 be my holding of,
daily make me harder
 hope and dearer love.

O thou our reminder
 of Christ crucified,
living Bread, the life of
 us for whom he died,
lend this life to me then;
 feed and feast my mind,
there be thou the sweetness
 man was meant to find.

Jesu, whom I look at
  shrouded here below,
I beseech thee send me
  what I long for so,
some day to gaze on thee
  face to face in light
and be blest for ever
  with thy glory's sight.

Ascribed to St Thomas Aquinas (1227-1274)
tr. Gerard Manley Hopkins

✦

O saving victim, opening wide
  The gate of heaven to man below,
Our foes press hard on every side:
  Thine aid supply, thy strength bestow.

All praise and thanks to thee ascend
  For evermore, blest One in Three;
O grant us life that shall not end
  In our true native land with thee. Amen.

St Thomas Aquinas (1227-1274)
tr. J.M. Neale & E. Caswall

✦

Of the glorious body telling,
O my tongue, its myst'ries sing,
and the blood, all price excelling,
which the world's eternal king,

in a noble womb once dwelling,
shed for this world's ransoming.

Giv'n for us, for us descending,
of a virgin to proceed,
man with man in converse blending,
scattered he the gospel seed,
till his sojourn drew to ending,
which he closed in wondrous deed.

At the last great supper lying,
circled by his brethren's band,
meekly with the law complying,
first, he finished its command.
Then, immortal food supplying,
gave himself with his own hand.

Word made flesh, by word he maketh
very bread his flesh to be,
Man in wine Christ's blood partaketh,
and if senses fail to see,
faith alone the true heart waketh,
to behold the mystery.

Therefore, we before him bending,
this great sacrament revere;
types and shadows have their ending,
for the newer rite is here;
faith, our outward sense befriending,
makes the inward vision clear.

Glory let us give, and blessing,
to the Father and the Son,

honour, might and praise addressing,
while eternal ages run;
ever too his love confessing,
who from both, with both is one.

St Thomas Aquinas (1227-1274)
tr. J.M. Neale, E. Caswall and others

To the Holy Spirit

Come, Holy Ghost, Creator, come
    from thy bright heavenly throne.
Come, take possession of our souls,
    and make them all thine own.

Thou who art called the Paraclete,
    best gift of God above,
the living spring, the living fire,
    sweet unction and true love.

Thou who are seven-fold in thy grace,
    finger of God's right hand;
his promise, teaching little ones
    to speak and understand.

O guide our minds with thy blest light,
    with love our hearts inflame;
and with thy strength, which ne'er decays,
    confirm our mortal frame.

Far from us drive our deadly foe;
    true peace unto us bring;
and through all perils lead us safe
    beneath thy sacred wing.

Through thee may we the Father know,
　　through thee th' eternal Son,
and thee the Spirit of them both,
　　thrice-blessed Three in One.

All glory to the Father be,
　　with his co-equal Son:
the same to thee great Paraclete,
　　while endless ages run.

Ascribed to Rabanus Maurus (776-856)
tr. Unknown

◆

Come, thou, Holy Spirit, come,
And from thy celestial home
　　Send thy light and brilliancy:
Father of the poor, draw near;
Giver of all gifts, be here;
　　Come, the soul's true radiancy.

Thou of comforters the best,
Thou the soul's most welcome guest,
　　Sweet refreshment here below;
In our labour rest most sweet,
Grateful coolness in the heat,
　　Solace in the aims of woe.

O most blessed light divine,
Shine within these hearts of thine,
　　And our inmost being fill;
Where thou are not, man hath nought,

Nothing good in deed or thought,
    Nothing free from taint of ill.

Heal our wounds; our strength renew;
On our dryness pour thy dew;
    Wash the stains of guilt away:
Bend the stubborn heart and will;
Melt the frozen, warm the chill;
    Guide the steps that go astray.

On the faithful, who adore
And confess thee, evermore
    In thy sevenfold gifts descend:
Give them virtue's sure reward,
Give them thy salvation, Lord,
    Give them joys that never end.

Veni, Sancte Spiritus
tr. E. Caswall & J.M. Neale

To the Blessed Virgin Mary

Bring flowers of the rarest,
bring blossoms the fairest,
from garden and woodland and hillside
    and dale;
our full hearts are swelling,
our glad voices telling
the praise of the loveliest flower of the vale.

O Mary, we crown thee with blossoms today,
Queen of the Angels and Queen of the May.(2)

Their lady they name thee,
their mistress proclaim thee.
Oh, grant that thy children on earth be as true
as long as the bowers
are radiant with flowers,
as long as the azure shall keep its bright hue.

Sing gaily in chorus,
the bright angels o'er us
re-echo the strains we begin upon earth;
their harps are repeating
the notes of our greeting,
for Mary herself is the cause of our mirth.

Author unknown

♦

Daily, daily, sing to Mary,
sing, my soul, her praises due;
all her feasts, her actions worship,
with her heart's devotion true.
Lost in wond'ring contemplation
be her majesty confessed:
call her Mother, call her Virgin,
happy Mother, Virgin blest.

She is mighty to deliver;
call her, trust her lovingly.
When the tempest round thee,
she will calm the troubled sea.
Gifts of heaven she has given,
noble Lady, to our race:

she, the Queen, who decks her subjects,
with the light of God's own grace.

Sing, my tongue, the Virgin's trophies,
who for us her Maker bore;
for the curse of old inflicted,
peace and blessings to restore.
Sing in songs of praise unending,
sing the world's majestic Queen;
weary not nor faint in telling
all the gifts she gives to men.

All my senses, heart, affections,
strive to sound her glory forth;
spread abroad, the sweet memorials,
of the Virgin's priceless worth.
Where the voice of music thrilling,
where the tongues of eloquence,
that can utter hymns beseeming
all her matchless excellence?

All our joys do flow from Mary,
all then join her praise to sing;
trembling, sing the Virgin Mother,
Mother of our Lord and King,
while we sing her awful glory,
far above our fancy's reach,
let our hearts be quick to offer
love the heart alone can reach.

Ascribed to St Bernard of Cluny (12th cenntury)
tr. H. Bittleston

◆

Hail, Queen of heav'n, the ocean star,
guide of the wand'rer here below;
thrown on life's surge, we claim thy care;
save us from peril and from woe.
Mother of Christ, star of the sea,
pray for the wanderer, pray for me.

O gentle, chaste and spotless maid,
we sinners make our prayers through thee;
remind thy Son that he has paid
the price of our iniquity.
Virgin most pure, star of the sea,
pray for the sinner, pray for me.

Sojourners in this vale of tears,
to thee, blest advocate, we cry;
pity our sorrows, calm our fears,
and soothe with hope our misery.
Refuge in grief, star of the sea,
pray for the mourner, pray for me.

And while to him who reigns above,
in Godhead One, in Persons Three,
the source of life, of grace, of love,
homage we pay on bended knee,
do thou, bright Queen, star of the sea,
pray for thy children, pray for me.

John Lingard (1771-1851)

♦

I'll sing a hymn to Mary,
   the Mother of my God,
the Virgin of all virgins,
   of David's royal blood.
O teach me, holy Mary,
   a loving song to frame,
when wicked men blaspheme thee,
   to love and bless thy name.

O noble Tower of David,
   of gold and ivory,
the Ark of God's own promise,
   the gate of heav'n to me,
to live and not to love thee
   would fill my soul with shame;
when wicked men blaspheme thee,
   I'll love and bless thy name.

The saints are high in glory,
   with golden crowns so bright;
but brighter far is Mary,
   upon her throne of light.
O that which God did give thee,
   let mortal ne'er disclaim;
when wicked men blaspheme thee
   I'll love and bless thy name.

But in the crown of Mary,
   there lies a wondrous gem,
as Queen of all the angels,
   which Mary shares with them:
no sin hath e'er defiled thee,
   so doth our faith proclaim;

when wicked men blaspheme thee
   I'll love and bless thy name.

John Wyse (1825-1898)

♦

Immaculate Mary! our hearts are on fire,
that title so wondrous fills all our desire.

Ave, ave, ave Maria! (twice)

We pray for God's glory, may his kingdom
   come!
We pray for his vicar, our Father, and Rome.

We pray for our mother the Church upon earth,
and bless, sweetest Lady, the land of our birth.

For poor, sick, afflicted thy mercy we crave;
and comfort the dying, thou light of the grave.

In grief and temptation, in joy or in pain,
we'll ask thee, our mother, nor seek thee
   in vain.

In death's solemn moment, our mother,
   be nigh:
as children of Mary, O teach us to die.

And crown thy sweet mercy with this
   special grace,
to behold soon in heaven God's ravishing face.

Now to God be all glory and worship for aye,
and to God's virgin mother an endless Ave.

Author unknown

O purest of creatures!
    Sweet mother, sweet maid:
the one spotless womb
    wherein Jesus was laid.
Dark night hath come down
    on us, mother, and we
look out for thy shining,
    sweet star of the sea.

Earth gave him one lodging;
    'twas deep in thy breast,
and God found a home where
    the sinner finds rest;
his home and his hiding place,
    both were in thee;
he was one by thy shining,
    sweet star of the sea.

Oh, blissful and calm
    was the wonderful rest
that thou gavest thy God
    in thy virginal breast;
for the heaven he left
    he found heaven in thee,
and he shone in thy shining,
    sweet star of the sea.

Frederick William Faber (1814-1863)

At the cross her station keeping,
stood the mournful mother weeping,
close to Jesus to the last.

Through her heart, his sorrow sharing,
all his better anguish bearing,
now at length the sword has passed.

Oh, how sad and sore distress'd
was that mother highly blest,
of the sole-begotten One.

Christ above in torment hangs;
she beneath beholds the pangs
of her dying glorious Son.

Is there one who would not weep,
whelm'd in miseries so deep,
Christ's dear mother to behold?

Can the human heart refrain
from partaking in her pain,
in that mother's pain untold?

Bruised, derided, cursed, defiled,
she beheld her tender child,
all with bloody scourges rent;

For the sins of his own nation,
saw him hang in desolation,
till his spirit forth he sent.

O thou mother! fount of love!
Touch my spirit from above,
make my heart with thine accord:

Make feel as thou hast felt;
make my soul to glow and melt
with the love of Christ my Lord.

Holy mother, pierce me through,
in my heart each wound renew
of my Saviour crucified.

Let me share with thee his pain
who for all my sins was slain,
who for me in torments died.

Let me mingle tears with thee,
mourning him who mourned for me,
all the days that I may live:

By the cross with thee to stay,
there with thee to weep and pray,
is all I ask of thee to give.

Ascribed to Jacopone da Todi (d. 1306)
tr. E. Caswall

For Christmas

Angels we have heard on high
sweetly singing o'er our plains,
and the mountains in reply
echo still their joyous strains.

Gloria in excelsis Deo.

Shepherds, why this jubilee?
Why your rapturous strain prolong?

Say, what may your tidings be,
which inspire your heavenly song.

Come to Bethlehem and see
him whose birth the angels sing:
come, adore on bended knee
the infant Christ, the new-born King.

See within a manger laid,
Jesus, Lord of heaven and earth!
Mary, Joseph, lend your aid
to celebrate our Saviour's birth.

James Chadwick (1813-1882)

♦

Come, come, come to the manger,
children, come to the children's King;
sing, sing, chorus of angels,
star of morning o'er Bethlehem sing.

He lies 'mid the beasts of the stall,
who is Maker and Lord of us all;
the wintry wind blows cold and dreary,
see, he weeps, the world is weary;
  Lord, have pity and mercy on me!

He leaves all his glory behind,
to be born and to die for mankind,
with grateful beasts his cradle chooses,
thankless man his love refuses;
  Lord, have pity and mercy on me!

To the manger of Bethlehem come,
to the Saviour Emmanuel's home;
the heavenly hosts above are singing,
set the Christmas bells a-ringing;
    Lord, have pity and mercy on me!

✦

Hark, the herald angels sing,
glory to the new-born king;
peace on earth and mercy mild,
God and sinners reconciled:
joyful all ye nations rise,
join the triumph of the skies,
with the angelic host proclaim,
Christ is born in Bethlehem.

Hark, the herald angels sing,
Glory to the new-born King.

Christ, by highest heaven adored,
Christ, the everlasting Lord,
late in time behold him come,
offspring of a Virgin's womb!
Veiled in flesh the Godhead see,
hail the Incarnate Deity!
Pleased as man with man to dwell,
Jesus, our Emmanuel.

Hail the heaven-born Prince of peace!
Hail the Son of righteousness!
Light and life to all he brings

risen with healing in his wings;
mild he lays his glory by,
born that man no more may die,
born to raise the sons of earth,
born to give them second birth.

> C. Wesley (1743), G. Whitefield (1753),
> M. Madan (1760), and others

◆

O come, all ye faithful,
joyful and triumphant,
O come ye, O come ye to Bethlehem;
come and behold him,
born the king of angels:

O come, let us adore him (three times)
Christ the Lord.

God of God,
light of light,
lo! he abhors not the virgin's womb;
very God,
begotten not created:

Sing, choirs of angels,
sing in exultation,
sing all ye citizens of heaven above:
glory to God
in the highest:

Yea, Lord, we greet thee,
born this happy morning,

Jesu, to thee be glory given;
Word of the Father,
now in flesh appearing.

John Wade (d. 1786)
tr. F. Oakley

♦

Once in royal David's city
stood a lowly cattle shed,
    where a Mother laid her Baby
    in a manger for his bed:
Mary was that Mother mild,
Jesus Christ her little child.

He came down to earth from heaven,
who is God and Lord of all,
    and his shelter was a stable
    and his cradle was a stall;
with the poor, and meek, and lowly,
lived on earth our Saviour holy.

And through all his wondrous childhood
he would honour and obey,
    love, and watch the lowly maiden
    in whose gentle arms he lay;
Christian children, all must be
mild, obedient, good as he.

For he is our childhood's pattern,
day by day like us he grew;
    he was little, weak and helpless,
    tears and smiles like us he knew;

and he feeleth for our sadness,
and he shareth in our gladness.

And our eyes at last shall see him
through his own redeeming love,
>   for that child so dear and gentle
>   is our Lord in heaven above;
and he leads his children on
to the place where he is gone.

Not in that poor lowly stable,
with the oxen standing by,
>   we shall see him; but in heaven,
>   set at God's right hand on high;
when like stars his children crowned
all in white shall wait around.

Cecil Frances Alexander (1818-1895)

◆

Silent night, holy night,
All is calm, all is bright,
round yon virgin mother and child;
holy infant so tender and mild:
>   sleep in heavenly peace,
>   sleep in heavenly peace.

Silent night, holy night.
Shepherds quake at the sight,
glories stream from heaven afar,
heavenly hosts sing alleluia:
>   Christ the Saviour is born,
>   Christ the Saviour is born.

Silent night, holy night.
Son of God, love's pure light
radiant beams from thy holy face,
with the dawn of redeeming grace:
> Jesus, Lord, at thy birth,
> Jesus, Lord, at thy birth.

Joseph Mohr (1792-1848)
tr. J. Young

◆

The first Noel the angel did say
was to certain poor shepherds in fields as
   they lay:
in fields as they lay keeping their sheep,
on a cold winter's night that was so deep.

> Noel, Noel, Noel, Noel,
> born is the King of Israel!

They lookèd up and saw a star,
shining in the east, beyond them far,
and to the earth it gave great light,
and so it continued both day and night.

And by the light of that same star,
three wise men came from country far.
to seek for a king was their intent,
and to follow the star wherever it went.

This star drew nigh to the north west,
o'er Bethlehem it took its rest,

and there it did both stop and stay
right over the place where Jesus lay.

Then entered in those wise men three,
full reverently upon their knee,
and offered there in his presence,
their gold and myrrh and frankincense.

Then let us all with one accord
sing praises to our heavenly Lord,
that hath made heaven and earth of nought,
and with his blood mankind hath bought.

Thomas Kelly (1769-1855)

General

Faith of our fathers, living still
   in spite of dungeon, fire and sword;
oh, how our hearts beat high with joy
   whene'er we hear that glorious word!

> Faith of our fathers! Holy faith!
> We will be true to thee till death,
> we will be true to thee till death.

Our fathers chained in prison dark,
   were still in heart and conscience free;
how sweet would be their children's fate,
   if they, like them, could die for thee!

Faith of our fathers, Mary's prayers
   shall win our country back to thee;

and through the truth that comes from God
   our land shall then indeed be free.

Faith of our fathers, we will love
   both friend and foe in all our strife,
and preach thee too, as love knows how,
   by kindly words and virtuous life.

Frederick William Faber (1814-1863)

❖

Lead, kindly light, amid encircling gloom,
   Lead thou me on;
The night is dark, and I am far from home,
   Lead thou me on.
Keep thou my feet; I do not ask to see
The distant scene; one step enough for me.

I was not ever thus, nor prayed that thou
   shouldst lead me on;
I loved to choose and see my path; but now
   Lead thou me on.
I loved the garish day, and, spite of fears,
Pride ruled my will: remember not past years.

So long thy power hath blessed me, sure it still
   will lead me on,
O'er moor and fen, o'er crag and torrent, till
   the night is gone;
And with the moon those angel faces smile,
Which I have loved long since, and lost awhile.

John Henry Newman (1801-1890)

Mine eyes have seen the glory
  of the coming of the Lord.
He is trampling out the vintage
  where the grapes of wrath are stored.
He has loosed the fateful lightning
  of his terrible swift sword.
His truth is marching on.

> Glory, glory, halleluja! Glory, glory, halleluja!
>   Glory, glory, halleluja!
> His truth is marching on.

I have seen him in the watch fires
  of a hundred circling camps.
They have gilded him an altar
  in the evening dews and damps.
I can read his righteous sentence
  by the dim and flaring lamps,
His day is marching on.

He has sounded forth the trumpet
  that shall never sound retreat.
He is sifting out the hearts of men
  before his judgement seat.
O, be swift my soul to answer him,
  be jubilant my feet!
Our God is marching on.

In the beauty of the lilies
  Christ was born across the sea

with a glory in his bosom
   that transfigures you and me.
As he died to make men holy,
   let us die to make men free,
Whilst God is marching on.

Julia Ward Howe (1719-1910)

◆

Nearer, my God, to thee,
   Nearer to thee!
E'en though it be a cross
   That raiseth me,
Still all my song would be,
Nearer, my God, to thee,
   Nearer to thee.

Though, like the wanderer,
   The sun gone down,
Darkness be over me,
   My rest a stone;
Yet in my dreams I'd be
Nearer, my God, to thee,
   Nearer to thee.

There let my way appear
   Steps unto heaven;
All that thou send'st to me
   In mercy given,
Angels to beckon me
Nearer, my God, to thee,
   Nearer to thee.

Then, with my waking thoughts
    Bright with thy praise,
Out of my stony griefs
    Bethel I'll raise;
So by my woes to be
Nearer, my God, to thee,
    Nearer to thee.

Sarah Flower Adams (1805-1848)

◆

Sing, my tongue, the glorious battle,
sing the last, the dread affray;
    o'er the cross, the victor's trophy,
    sound the high triumphal lay;
how, the pains of death enduring,
earth's redeemer won the day.

Faithful cross! above all other,
one and only noble tree!
    None in foliage, none in blossom,
    none in fruit thy peer may be;
sweetest wood and sweetest iron!
sweetest weight is hung on thee.

Bend, O lofty tree, thy branches,
thy too rigid sinews bend;
    and awhile the stubborn hardness,
    which thy birth bestowed, suspend;
and the limbs of heaven's high monarch
gently on thine arms extend.

Thou alone wast counted worthy
this world's ransom to sustain,

that by thee a wrecked creation
    might its ark and haven gain,
with the sacred blood anointed
of the Lamb that hath been slain.

Praise and honour to the Father,
praise and honour to the Son,
    praise and honour to the Spirit,
    ever three and ever one,
one in might and one in glory,
while eternal ages run.

Venantius Fortunatus (530-609)
tr. J.M. Neale

◆

The royal banners forward go,
    the cross shines forth in mystic glow,
where he in flesh, our flesh who made,
    our sentence bore, our ransom paid.

There, whilst he hung, his sacred side
    by soldier's spear was open'd wide,
to cleanse us in the precious flood
    of water mingled with his blood.

Fulfill'd is now what David told
    in true prophetic song of old,
how God the heathen's king should be;
    for God is reigning from the tree.

O tree of glory, tree most fair,
    ordain'd those holy limbs to bear,

how bright in purple robe it stood,
  the purple of a saviour's blood!

Upon its arms, like balance true,
  he weighed the price for sinners due,
the price which none but he could pay:
  and spoil'd the spoiler of his prey.

To thee, eternal Three in One,
  let homage meet by all be done,
as by the cross thou dost restore,
  so rule and guide us evermore.

Venantius Fortunatus (530-609)
tr. J.M. Neale and others

♦

When I survey the wondrous Cross
  On which the Prince of glory died,
My richest gain I count but loss,
  And pour contempt on all my pride.

Forbid it, Lord, that I should boast
  Save in the death of Christ, my God;
All the vain things that charm me most,
  I sacrifice them to his blood.

See, from his head, his hands, his feet,
  Sorrow and love flow mingled down;
Did e'er such love and sorrow meet,
  Or thorns compose so rich a crown?

Were the whole realm of nature mine,
  That were an offering far too small;

LATIN HYMNS

Adoro te devote latens Deitas,
quae sub his figuris vere latitas;
tibi se cor meum, totum subiicit,
quia te contemplans totum deficit.

Visus, tactus, gustus in te fallitur,
sed auditu solo tuto creditur;
credo quidquid dixit Dei filius:
Nihil hoc verbo veritatis verius.

In cruce latebat sola Deitas,
at hic latet simul et humanitas:
ambo tamen credens atque confitens,
peto quod petivit latro poenitens.

Plagas, sicut Thomas, non intueor,
Deum tamen meum te confiteor,
fac me tibi semper magis credere,
in te spem habere, te diligere.

O memoriale mortis Domini,
Panis vivus vitam praestans homini,
praesta meae menti de te vivere,
et te illi semper dulce sapere.

Pie pelicane, Iesu Domine,
me immundum munda tuo sanguine,
cuius una stilla salvum facere
totum mundum quit ab omni scelere.

Iesu, quem velatum nunc adspicio,
oro fiat illud quod tam sitio:
ut te revelata cernens facie,
visu sim beatus tuae gloriae. Amen.

◆

Anima Christi, sanctifica me;
Corpus Christi, salva me;
Sanguis Christi, inebria me;
Aqua lateris Christi, lava me;
Passio Christi, conforta me;
O bone Iesu, exaudi me.

Intra vulnera tua, absconde me;
ne permittas me separari a te;
ab hoste maligno defende me;
in hora mortis meae voca me;
et iube me venire ad te;
ut cum sanctis tuis laudem te
per infinita saecula saeculorum. Amen.

◆

Ave verum Corpus natum
de Maria Virgine;
vere passum immolatum
in cruce pro homine.

Cuius latus perforatum
fluxit aqua et sanguine:
esto nobis praegustatum
mortis in examine.

O Iesu dulcis!
O Iesu pie!
O Iesu, fili Mariae!

✦

Cor dulce, cor amabile,
amore nostri saucium,
amore nostri languidum,
fac sis mihi placabile.

Cor Iesu melle dulcius,
Cor sole puro purius,
Templi Dei sacrarium,
Opum Dei compendium.

Tu portus orbi naufrago,
Secura pax fidelibus,
Reis asilum mentibus
piis recessus cordibus. Amen.

Ecce panis angelorum
factus cibus viatorum:
vere panis filiorum,
non mittendus canibus.

In figuris praesignatur:
cum Isaac immolatur,
Agnus Paschae deputatur,
datur manna patribus.

Bone Pastor, panis vere,
Iesu, nostri miserere,
tu nos pasce, nos tuere,

tu nos bona fac videre
in terra viventium.

Tu, qui cuncta scis et vales,
qui nos pascis hic mortales,
tuos ibi commensales;
coheredes et sodales
fac sanctorum civium. Amen.

✦

Gloria in excelsis Deo
et in terra pax hominibus bonae voluntatis.
Laudamus te,
benedicimus te,
adoramus te,
glorificamus te,
gratias agimus tibi propter magnam gloriam
   tuam,
Domine Deus, Rex caelestis,
Deus Pater omnipotens.
Domine Filii unigenite, Iesu Christe,
Domine Deus, Agnus Dei, Filius Patris,
qui tollis peccata mundi, miserere nobis;
qui tollis peccata mundi, suscipe deprecationem
   nostram.
Qui sedes ad dexteram Patris, miserere nobis.
Quoniam tu solus Sanctus, tu solus Dominus,
tu solus Altissimus,
Iesu Christe, cum Sancto Spiritu: in gloria
   Dei Patris. Amen.

✦

Gloria Patri, et Filio, et Spiritui Sancto.
Sicut erat in principio, et nunc, et semper,
et in saecula saeculorum. Amen.

✦

Iesu dulcis memoria,
Dans vera cordis gaudia:
Sed super mel et omnia,
Eius dulcis praesentia.

Nil canitur suavius,
Nil auditur iucundius,
Nil cogitatur dulcius,
Quam Iesus Dei Filius.

Iesu, spes poenitentibus,
Quam pius es petentibus!
Quam bonus te quaerentibus!
Sed quid invenientibus?

Nec lingua valet dicere,
Nec littera exprimere:
Expertus potest credere,
Quid sit Iesum diligere.

Sis Iesu nostrum gaudium,
qui es futurus praemium:
Sit nostra in te gloria,
Per cuncta semper secula. Amen.

✦

Magnificat anima mea Dominum;
Et exsultavit spiritus meus in Deo salvatore meo,
Quia respexit humilitatem ancillae suae:
    ecce enim ex hoc beatam me dicent omnes
        generationes,
Quia fecit mihi magna qui potens est,
    et sanctum nomen eius,
Et misericordia eius a progenie in progenies
    timentibus eum.
Fecit potentiam bracchio suo;
    dispersit superbos mente cordis sui.
Deposuit potentes de sede, et exaltavit humiles.
Suscepit Israel, servum suum,
    recordatus misericordiæ suæ,
Sicut locutus est ad patres nostros,
    Abraham et semen eius in sæcula.
Gloria Patri, et Filio, et Spiritui Sancto.
Sicut erat in principio, et nunc, et semper,
    et in sæcula sæculorum. Amen.

✦

O sacrum convivium! in quo Christus
sumitur: recolitur memoria passionis eius:
mens impletur gratia,
et futurae gloriae
nobis pignus datur, alleluia.

✦

Pange lingua gloriosi
Corporis mysterium
Sanguinisque pretiosi,
Quem in mundi pretium
Fructus ventris generosi
Rex effudit gentium.

Nobis datus, nobis natus
Ex intacta Virgine,
Et in mundo conversatus,
Sparso verbi semine,
Sui moras incolatus
Miro clausit ordine.

In supremae nocte coenae
Recumbens cum fratribus,
Observata lege plene
Cibis in legalibus,
Cibum turbae duodenae
Se dat suis manibus.

Verbum caro, panem verum
Verbo carnem efficit:
Fitque Sanguis Christi merum,
Et si sensus deficit,
Ad firmandum cor sincerum
Sola fides sufficit.

Tantum ergo Sacramentum
Veneremur cernui:
Et antiquum documentum
Novo cedat ritui:
Praestet fides supplementum
Sensuum defectui.

Genitori, Genitoque
Laus et iubilatio,
Salus, honor, virtus quoque
Sit et benedictio;
Procedenti ab utroque
Compar sit laudatio. Amen.

◆

Pater noster, qui es in caelis:
sanctificetur nomen tuum;
adveniat regnum tuum;
fiat voluntas tua, sicut in caelo, et in terra.
Panem nostrum cotidianum da nobis hodie;
et dimitte nobis debita nostra,
sicut et nos dimittimus debitoribus nostris;
et ne nos inducas in tentationem;
sed libera nos a malo. Amen.

◆

Te Deum laudamus: te Dominum confitemur.
Te aeternum Patrem omnis terra veneratur.
Tibi omnes angeli, tibi caeli et universae
    potestates:
Tibi cherubim et seraphim incessabili voce
    proclamant:
Sanctus, sanctus, sanctus Dominus Deus
    Sabaoth.
Pleni sunt caeli et terra maiestatis gloriae tuae.
Te gloriosus apostolorum chorus:

Te prophetarum laudabilis numerus:
Te martyrum candidatus laudat exercitus.
Te per orbem terrarum sancta confitetur ecclesia:
Patrem immensae maiestatis:
Venerandum tuum verum et unicum Filium:
Sanctum quoque Paraclitum Spiritum.
Tu Rex gloriae, Christe.
Tu Patris sempiternus es Filius.
Tu ad liberandum suscepturus hominem, non horruisti Virginis uterum.
Tu devicto mortis aculeo, aperuisti credentibus regna caelorum.
Tu ad dexteram Dei sedes, in gloria Patris.
Iudex crederis esse venturus.
Te ergo quaesumus, tuis famulis subveni, quos pretioso sanguine redemisti.
Aeterna fac cum sanctis tuis in gloria numerari.
Salvum fac populum tuum Domine, et benedic haereditati tuae.
Et rege eos, et extolle illos usque in aeternum.
Per singulos dies benedicimus te.
Et laudamus nomen tuum in saeculum, et in saeculum saeculi.
Dignare Domine die isto sine peccato nos custodire.
Miserere nostri Domine, miserere nostri.
Fiat misericordia tua Domine super nos, quemadmodum speravimus in te.
In te Domine speravi, non confundar in aeternum.

✦

Ubi caritas et amor, Deus ibi est.

Congregavit nos in unum Christi amor.
Exsultemus, et in ipso iucundemur.
Timeamus et amemus Deum vivum.
Et ex corde diligamus nos sincero.

Ubi caritas et amor, Deus ibi est.

Simul ergo cum in unum congregamur:
Ne nos mente dividamus caveamus.
Cessent iurgia maligna, cessent lites.
Et in medio nostri sit Christus Deus.

Ubi caritas et amor, Deus ibi est.

Simul quoque cum beatis videamus.
Glorianter vultum tuum, Christe Deus:
Gaudium quod est immensum atque probum,
Saecula per infinita saeculorum. Amen.

✦

Veni Creator Spiritus,
Mentes tuorum visita:
Imple superna gratia
Quae tu creasti pectora.

Qui diceris Paraclitus,
Altissimi donum Dei,
Fons vivus ignis caritas,
Et spiritalis unctio.

Tu septiformis munere,
Digitus paternae dexterae,
Tu rite promissum Patris,
Sermone ditans guttura.

Accende lumen sensibus,
Infunde amorem cordibus,
Infirma nostri corporis
Virtute firmans perpeti.

Hostem repellas longius,
Pacemque dones protinus:
Ductore sic te praevio,
Vitemus omne noxium.

Per te sciamus da Patrem,
Noscamus atque Filium,
Teque utriusque Spiritum
Credamus omni tempore.

Deo Patri sit gloria,
Et Filio qui a mortuis
Surrexit ac Paraclito,
In saeculorum saecula. Amen.

◆

Veni Sancte Spiritus,
Et emitte caelitus
Lucis tuae radium.

Veni pater pauperum,
Veni dator munerum,
Veni lumen cordium.

Consolator optime,
Dulcis hospes animae,
Dulce refrigerium.

In labore requies,
In aestu temperies,
In fletu solatium.

O lux beatissima,
Reple cordis intima
Tuorum fidelium.

Sine tuo numine,
Nihil est in homine,
Nihil est innoxium.

Lava quod est sordidum,
Riga quod est aridum,
Sana quod est saucium.

Flecte quod est rigidum,
Fove quod est frigidum,
Rege quod est devium.

Da tuis fidelibus,
In te connfidentibus,
Sacrum septenarium.

Da virtutis meritum,
Da salutis exitum,
Da perenne gaudium. Amen.

✦

Vexilla Regis prodeunt:
Fulget crucis mysterium,
Qua vita mortem pertulit,
Et morte vitam protulit.

Quae vulnerata lanceae
Mucrone diro, criminum
Ut nos lavaret sordibus,
Manavit unda et sanguine.

Impleta sunt quae concinit
David fideli carmine,
Dicendo nationibus:
Regnavit a ligno Deus.

Arbor decora et fulgida,
Ornata Regis purpura,
Electa digno stipite
Tam sancta membra tangere.

Beata, cuius brachiis
Pretium pependit saeculi:
Statera facta corporis,
Tulitque praedam tartari.

O Crux ave, spes unica,
Hoc passionis tempore
Piis adauge gratiam,
Reisque dele crimina.

Te fons salutis Trinitas,
Collaudet omnis spiritus:
Quibus crucis victoriam
Largiris adde praemium. Amen.

✦

Victimae paschali laudes
Immolent Christiani.
Agnus redemit oves:
Christus innocens Patri
Reconciliavit peccatores.

Mors et vita duello
Conflixere mirando:
Dux vitae mortuus,
Regnat vivus.

Dic nobis Maria,
Quid vidisti in via?
Sepulcrum Christi viventis,
Et gloriam vidi resurgentis:
Angelicos testes,
Sudarium et vestes.

Surrexit Christus spes mea:
Praecedet suos in Galilaeam.
Scimus Christum surrexisse
A mortuis vere:
Tu nobis, victor Rex, miserere. Amen. (Alleluia.)

✦

Alma Redemptoris Mater,
Quae pervia coeli porta manes,
Et stella maris,
Succurre cadenti, surgere qui curat populo:

Tu quae genuisti, natura mirante,
Tuum sanctum Genitorem,
Virgo prius ac posterius,
Gabrielis ab ore sumens illud Ave,
Peccatorum miserere.

✦

Ave Maria,
gratia plena,
Dominus tecum.
Benedicta tu in mulieribus
et benedictus fructus ventris tui Jesus.
Sancta Maria,
Mater Dei,
ora pro nobis peccatoribus,
nunc et in hora mortis nostrae. Amen.

✦

Ave maris stella,
Dei Mater alma,
Atque semper virgo,
Felix caeli porta.

Sumens illud Ave
Gabrielis ore,
Funda nos in pace,
Mutans Hevae nomen.

Solve vincla reis,
Profer lumen caecis:
Mala nostra pelle
Bona cuncta posce.

Monstra te esse matrem:
Sumat per te preces,
Qui pro nobis natus,
Tulit esse tuus.

Virgo singularis,
Inter omnes mitis,
Nos culpis solutos,
Mites fac et castos.

Vitam praesta puram
Iter para tutum:
Ut videntes Iesum,
Semper collaetemur.

Sit laus Deo Patri,
Summo Christo decus,
Spiritui Sancto,
Tribus honor unus. Amen.

✦

Ave, Regina coelorum,
Ave, Domina Angelorum:
Salve, radix, salve, porta,
Ex qua mundo lux est orta.

Gaude, Virgo gloriosa,
Super omnes speciosa;
Vale, O valde decora,
Et pro nobis Christum exora.

✦

Salve, Regina, mater misericordiae,
Vita, dulcedo, et spes nostra, salve.
Ad te clamamus, exsules filii Hevae.
Ad te suspiramus, gementes et flentes
    in hac lacrimarm valle.
Eia ergo, advocata nostra,
Illos tuos misericordes oculos
    ad nos converte.
Et Iesum, benedictum fructum ventris tui,
    nobis post hoc exilium ostende.
O clemens, O pia, O dulcis
Virgo Maria.

◆

Stabat Mater dolorosa
Iuxta crucem lacrimosa,
Dum pendebat Filius.

Cuius animam gementem,
Contristatam et dolentem
Pertransivit gladius.

O quam tristis et afflicta
Fuit illa benedicta
Mater unigeniti!

Quae maerebat et dolebat,
Pia Mater, dum videbat
Nati poenas inclyti.

Quis est homo qui non fleret,
Matrem Christi si videret
In tanto supplicio?

Quis non potest contristari,
Christi Matrem contemplari
Dolentem cum Filio?

Pro peccatis suae gentis,
Vidit Iesum in tormentis,
Et flagellis subditum.

Vidit suum dulcem natum
Moriendo desolatum,
Dum emisit spiritum.

Eia Mater fons amoris,
Me sentire vim doloris
Fac, ut tecum lugeam.

Fac ut ardeat cor meum
In amando Christum Deum,
Ut sibi complaceam.

Sancta Mater, istud agas,
Crucifixi fige plagas
Cordi meo valide.

Tui nati vulnerati,
Tam dignati pro me pati,
Poenas mecum divide.

Fac me tecum pie flere,
Crucifixo condolere,
Donec ego vixero.

Iuxta crucem tecum stare,
Et me tibi sociare
In planctu desidero.

Virgo virginum praeclara,
Mihi iam non sis amara:
Fac me tecum plangere.

Fac ut portem Christi mortem
Passionis fac consortem,
Et plagas recolere.

Fac me plagis vulnerari,
Fac me cruce inebriari,
Et cruore Filii.

Flammis ne urar succensus,
Per te, virgo, sim defensus
In die iudicii.

Christe, cum sit hinc exire,
Da per Matrem me venire
Ad palmam victoriae.

Quando corpus morietur,
Fac ut animae donetur
Paradisi gloria. Amen.

◆

Sub tuum praesidium confugimus,
Sancta Dei Genitrix,
nostras deprecationes ne despicias,
in necessitatibus nostris,
sed a periculis cunctis libera nos semper,
Virgo gloriosa et benedicta.

◆

INDEX

DAILY PRAYERS

Act of Contrition	14
Act of Faith	13
Act of Hope	13
Act of Love	13
Angelus	8
Apostles' Creed	10
Before Study	15
Before Work	15
Confiteor	18
Creed (*see:* Apostles' Creed, Nicene Creed)	10
Gloria	14
Glory Be	8
Grace after Meals	15
Grace before Meals	15
Guardian Angel	10
Hail Mary	7
I confess (*see:* Confiteor)	18
Lord's Prayer, The	7
Morning Prayer	10
Nicene Creed	11
Night Prayer	18
Our Father (*see:* Lord's Prayer)	7
Prayer of Adoration	9
Prayer for a Happy Death	18
Prayer for final Perseverance	17
Prayer to Jesus Christ	16

Prayer to the Holy Spirit	17
Queen of Heaven (*see:* Regina Coeli)	9
Reading the Bible (Before)	16
Reading the Bible (After)	16
Regina Coeli	9
Sign of the cross	7

GENERAL PRAYERS

Deliver us, Lord	19
For Christian Unity	25
For civil authorities	27
For community spirit	21
For love of Neighbour	19
For our country	27
For peace and justice	20
For persecuted Christians	25
For prisoners	22
For refugees	22
For sharing	20
For the Church	24
For the dead	28
For the handicapped	23
For the homeless	23
For the local Church	24
For the media apostolate	27
For the missions	26
For the Pope	25
For vocations	26
For work	21
God be in my head	19
Master's Way	28

Prayers to Jesus

Be thou a light	36
Before Mass	38
Before the Blessed Sacrament	38
Behold, O kind and most sweet Jesus	35
(*see:* Prayer before a Crucifix)	40
Christ be near	30
Come, my way	29
Eucharistic offering	40
Give me, good Lord	32
Hymn to Christ	41
Jesus, Divine Master	29
Lord, give me patience	34
Lord Jesus Christ	29
Lord Jesus, I give you	30
Lord, make me an instrument	32
O blessed Jesus	31
O Lord and Master	37
Prayer before a Crucifix	40
Prayer of self-dedication to Jesus Christ	34
Set our hearts on fire	35
Soul of Christ (*see:* Anima Christi)	33
Teach us, Good Lord	31
Thanks be to you	34
Use me, my Saviour	36

Prayers to the Blessed Virgin Mary

Hail, Holy Queen	44
Memorare (*see:* Remember, O most gracious)	43

Prayer to Our Lady of Lourdes	44
Prayer to Our Lady of perpetual succour	45
Prayer to Our Lady, Queen of Apostles	45
Remember, O most gracious Virgin Mary	43
To the Immaculate Heart of Mary	46

PRAYERS TO THE SAINTS

Prayer to St Anthony	50
Prayer to St Brigid	51
Prayer to St Joseph	49
Prayer to St Jude	51
Prayer to St Martin	52
Prayer to St Oliver Plunkett	52
Prayer to St Patrick	53
Prayer to St Paul the Apostle	53
Prayer to St Rita	54
Prayer to St Teresa of the Child Jesus	54

LITANIES

Litany of the Most Holy Name of Jesus	57
Litany of the Sacred Heart	55
Litany of Our Lady	61
Litany of Saints	64

ROSARY 67

The Joyful Mysteries	68
The Sorrowful Mysteries	70
The Glorious Mysteries	73

BENEDICTION 77

STATIONS OF THE CROSS 81

PRAYERS FROM THE BIBLE 97

Blessed are you, O Lord God of our ancestors 97
Blessed are you, O Lord, 97
But you, O Lord, reign for ever 99
But you, our God, are kind and true 100
Have mercy on me, O God 101
Have regard to the prayer of thy servant 97
Heal me, O Lord 99
I have sinned, O Lord 103
My soul magnifies the Lord 103
O Lord, God of heaven 98
O Lord, you are our Father 99
Out of the depths I cry to you, O Lord 102
Praise the Lord, all you nations 102
Save us by your hand 98
The Lord is my strength 97
This is eternal life 104
You are worthy, our Lord and God 105
You have rescued me 99

HYMNS 107

TO GOD THE FATHER

All people that on earth do dwell 107
Amazing grace 108
God be with you 108
God of mercy and compassion 109

Now thank we all our God	110
Praise to the Holiest in the height	112
Praise to the Lord, the Almighty	113
Praise we our God with joy	113
The Lord's my shepherd	114

To Jesus

Abide with me	115
Godhead here in hiding	122
Jesus, my Lord, my God, my all	116
O bread of heaven	120
O saving victim, opening wide	124
Of the glorious body telling	124
Soul of my Saviour	117
Sweet Heart of Jesus	118
Sweet sacrament divine	121
To Jesus' Heart, all burning	119

To the Holy Spirit

Come, Holy Ghost, Creator, come	126
Come, thou Holy Spirit, come	127

To the Blessed Virgin Mary

At the cross her station keeping	135
Bring flowers of the rarest	128
Daily, daily, sing to Mary	129
Hail, Queen of heav'n	131
I'll sing a hymn to Mary	132
Immaculate Mary!	133
O purest of creatures!	134

For Christmas

Angels we have heard on high	136
Come, come, come to the manger	137
Hark, the herald angels sing	138
O come, all ye faithful	139
Once in royal David's city	140
Silent night	141
The first Noel	142

General

Faith of our fathers	143
Lead, kindly light	144
Mine eyes have seen the glory	145
Nearer, my God, to thee	146
Sing, my tongue, the glorious battle	147
The royal banners forward go	148
When I survey the wondrous Cross	149

Latin hymns

Adoro te devote	151
Alma Redemptoris Mater	164
Anima Christi	152
Ave Maria	165
Ave maris stella	165
Ave Regina coelorum	166
Ave verum	152
Cor dulce, cor amabile	153
Gloria in excelsis	154
Gloria Patri	155
Iesu dulcis memoria	155

Magnificat	156
O Sacrum Courvivium	156
Pange lingua	157
Pater noster	158
Salve Regina	167
Stabat Mater	167
Sub tuum praesidium	169
Tantum ergo	157
Te Deum	158
Ubi caritas et amor	160
Veni Creator Spiritus	160
Veni Sancte Spiritus	161
Vexhilla Regis	163
Victimae Paschali laudes	164

HYMNS
(Title of First Line)

Abide with me	115
Adoro te devote	151
All people that on earth do dwell	107
Alma Redemptoris Mater	164
Amazing grace	108
Angels we have heard on high	136
Anima Christi	152
At the cross her station keeping	135
Ave Maria	165
Ave maris stella	165
Ave Regina coelorum	166
Ave verum	152
Bring flowers of the rarest	128
Come, come, come to the manger	137
Come, Holy Ghost, Creator, come	126
Come, thou Holy Spirit, come	127
Cor dulce, cor amabile	153
Daily, daily, sing to Mary	129
Faith of our fathers	143
Gloria in excelsis	154
Gloria Patri	155
God be with you	108
God of mercy and compassion	109
Godhead here in hiding	122
Hail, Queen of heav'n	131
Hark, the herald angels sing	138

I'll sing a hymn to Mary	132
Iesu dulcis memoria	155
Immaculate Mary!	333
Jesus, my Lord, my God, my all	116
Lead, kindly light	144
Magnificat	156
Mine eyes have seen the glory	145
Nearer, my God, to thee	146
Now thank we all our God	110
O bread of heaven	120
O come, all ye faithful	139
O purest of creatures!	134
O Sacrum Convivium	156
O saving victim, opening wide	124
Of the glorious body telling	124
Once in royal David's city	140
Pange lingua	157
Pater noster	158
Praise to the Holiest in the height	112
Praise to the Lord, the Almighty	113
Praise we our God with joy	113
Salve Regina	167
Silent night	141
Sing, my tongue, the glorious battle	147
Soul of my Saviour	117
Stabat Mater	167
Sub tuum praesidium	169
Sweet Heart of Jesus	118
Sweet sacrament divine	121
Tantum ergo	157
Te Deum	158

The first Noel	142
The Lord's my shepherd	114
The royal banners forward go	148
To Jesus' Heart, all burning	119
Ubi caritas et amor	160
Veni Creator Spiritus	160
Veni Sancte Spiritus	161
Vexhilla Regis	163
Victimae Paschali laudes	164
When I survey the wondrous Cross	149